Christian Maturity
& Christian Success

Christian Maturity
& Christian Success

Daniel Jenkins

FORTRESS PRESS   **Philadelphia**

LAITY EXCHANGE BOOKS

As noted in the text, biblical quotations are from the Authorized King James Version of the Bible (AV); the Revised Standard Version of the Bible (RSV), copyrighted 1946, 1952, © 1971, 1973 by the Division of Christian Education of the National Council of the Churches of Christ in the U.S.A.; and The New English Bible (NEB), © The Delegates of the Oxford University Press and The Syndics of the Cambridge University Press 1961, 1970, and are used by permission.

Chapters 1–3 and 9–12 first appeared in *Christian Maturity and the Theology of Success,* © 1976 SCM Press, London, and are reprinted here in slightly revised form by permission.

Library of Congress Cataloging in Publication Data

Jenkins, Daniel Thomas, 1914–
Christian maturity and Christian success.

(Laity exchange books)
1. Christian life—Reformed authors.
I. Title. II. Series.
BV4501.2.J42   1982   248.4   82–9759
ISBN 0–8006–1657–X   AACR2

9586D82   Printed in the United States of America   1-1657

Contents

Editor's Introduction

THERE ARE three special reasons why I am happy that we can include this book in our *Laity Exchange* series.

The topic is an important and neglected one. Many good committed Christian people are a little depressed and defeated these days. We hear much bad news; we sometimes feel vaguely guilty about not doing enough; we are not accustomed to think in terms of Christian "success"—and that itself is a sign of our spiritual immaturity. Daniel Jenkins makes us think hard about the possibilities and dangers of a successful life, not a weak and failing one.

And Professor Jenkins is particularly equipped to write for American readers. He is himself a product of that fiercely strong Welsh Protestant tradition which has contributed more than most people have noticed to both British and North American church life. He has been for many years a constant visitor to and teacher in the United States, including appointments as a visiting professor to the University of Chicago Divinity School and now as Professor of Systematic Theology at Princeton Theological Seminary. (We miss him in London, and envy Princeton.)

But perhaps the most important reason why this book is valuable is that all his life, whether in Wales or England or North America, Daniel Jenkins has known and taught and argued about the vocation and responsibilities of the laity. For some time he was general secretary of the Christian Frontier Council in London, that informal but influential group of "establishment" lay people founded by the great Dr. J. H. Oldham. I was myself a humble assistant editor of their journal *Frontier*, and I want to pay tribute to the fine quality of the

study groups and the writing projects that Professor Jenkins organized for the Frontier Council on such questions as medical ethics, the
quality of public education, and international affairs. These groups
informed both church and secular leaders in London with careful and
yet sharp critiques on current problems. It is with the same quality of
Christian thinking that he writes for us now.

MARK GIBBS

Faith and Success

Few people think readily in these days of any connection between Christian faith and what is commonly thought of as success. In European lands, churches have suffered from prolonged institutional decline, with the result that their leaders have not claimed much public attention and their theologians have become self-critical. Even in America, where the institutional situation is very different, professional theologians recoil in horror from anything which hints at the power of positive thinking. The dangers of ecclesiastical triumphalism, the attitude which does not make a sharp enough distinction between the kingdom of God and the earthly church, have been a staple theme of the ecumenical movement for over a generation. Nowadays, Roman Catholic theologians vie with those of the Reformed tradition in emphasizing that theirs is a theology of the cross rather than one of glory. Churchmen in Africa, Asia, and South America have been at pains to assert their solidarity with the poor, the dispossessed, and those struggling to obtain political power, and their influence has been dominant in the World Council of Churches in recent years. People outside the Christian community often think of the church as an institution on the defensive, whose representatives lack the self-confidence that comes from familiarity with the sweet smell of success.

This situation has regrettable consequences. Christians themselves come to think of maturity not as a present possession, a gift from their Lord, but as the object of vague aspiration, something seen only by contrast with the immaturity which is our normal state. This means that they give little attention to what follows after they have discovered and obeyed what they believe to be the will of God. This book will try to show that this both hinders them from making the most of resources they already possess and from facing the distinctive temptations to which they are exposed, those which arise from the successful fulfillment of their vocation.

A few recent theologians have hinted at a different approach, but they have done no more than that. Bonhoeffer has a short passage in his *Ethics* entitled "The Successful Man"[1] but, despite the extremely affirmative view of life and its possibilities under God which he was increasingly taking at that time, it deals mainly with the contrast between the crucified Christ and the world's understanding of success. Heinrich Ott, basing himself on Bonhoeffer, picks up the theme in his *Reality and Faith*[2] only to discard it without further discussion. Karl Barth, the outstanding systematic theologian of the last generation, is preeminently the theologian who sees Christian maturity in terms of success. His theology is rightly described by G. C. Berkouwer as that of "the triumph of grace."[3] We shall be drawing extensively in this discussion on those great quarries, still inadequately mined, of the third and fourth volumes of his major work, the *Church Dogmatics,* for a great deal of our material, but even he does not deal with the matter directly and ignores many of its aspects.[4]

The New Testament is, above all else, a success story. This is why the Gospels are given their name. They are good tidings of great joy. Yet it is a success very different from any which the world knows. It is won only through the most radical kind of apparent failure against the strongest of opponents, and it also confronts those who participate in this success with a whole new range of difficulties, which only become visible as a result of that success. The Gospels make little sense until it is seen that they are addressed primarily to believers, those who already share in a measure of the success of Christ, those who are, therefore, the rich, the heirs of the kingdom, who have begun to enjoy the glorious liberty of the children of God. It is only when this is grasped that the full originality of the Gospels' warnings against the perils of riches can be appreciated. The natural human temptation is to misunderstand these warnings by assuming that they must refer primarily to others rather than to ourselves, those who happen to be materially better off than we are or who have some position or privilege which we covet for ourselves or, more insidiously, for someone else whom we consider more deserving than their present possessors. But in this context such distinctions are trivial. Whatever his or her worldly circumstances, anyone who has the spirit of Christ and who is an heir of the eternal covenant is rich.[5] Our riches may be more spiritual than material and may themselves be the fruit of the purest faith, yet they remain riches, and the awful warning "how hardly shall they that have riches enter the kingdom of God" still speaks to our condition. This is true even though we are already the beneficiaries of the kingdom, in the way the rich young ruler himself was. Mature Christians are precisely those who know that they are rich and who enjoy their riches and become richer in the process. They also know that this makes their position before God all the more precarious, so that they are driven back constantly to the realization that all this is possible only through God's grace, made clear in the cross and resurrection of Jesus Christ.

This central truth in the teaching of Jesus concerning the kingdom is exemplified in the experience of the apostle Paul, whose letters are particularly revealing in this respect. Again, it is essential to realize that Paul is the rich man, the Hebrew of the Hebrews who is aware of being an heir of the promises made to Abraham. The self-consciousness that leads to an awareness of radical contradiction and that prompted him to develop the great argument of the first eight chapters of Romans, was the product not of weakness, of a slave mentality, but of the seriousness which comes from strength. It was Nietzsche's failure to see this which led him so completely to misunderstand Paul, whom he regarded as an outstanding example of the resentment which arises from spiritual failure.

Paul has the conscience of the rich, and he is trying to face the difficulties which arise because of the burden of riches. As with Job before him, these arise precisely because of his faithfulness to his vocation, and he is vindicated only because he refuses to allow them to make him forsake his vocation. The more seriously Paul tries to follow the God-given law, the deeper become his sense of responsibility and his moral insight, and the more aware he becomes of falling short. Grace comes to him as release from the existential tension caused by this apparently insoluble moral dilemma, but Paul would not have known this grace unless he had had the strength to face this

dilemma without flinching. When it does come in these circumstances, it is immensely creative, as the eighth chapter of Romans
makes so vividly clear. Yet, as the Corinthian church drives Paul
almost to despair by failing to see, it remains creative only if it
continues to be seen as grace, making us aware of the new dangers
which arise in consequence of the very victories which have been won
for us. Maturity has really been given to humankind. This is set forth
in the widest possible setting in the daring claims made by the letter to
the Ephesians. We have been set free and, as the letter to the Galatians insists, must never be content to settle for less than the full
freedom that maturity demands. But that freedom is not now a natural
possession. Because it is known only in Christ, it can only find
expression in constant struggle with all those forces which deny
Christ, both within ourselves and in our dealings with each other and
the world around us. As with all the workings of grace, we genuinely
possess this maturity, yet do so only as we overcome evidences of
immaturity or misuses of new-found power which arise as we move
further along the road to its full realization.

This is one reason why we need the guidance of the Spirit. The
Pauline writings are also notable for their emphasis on how necessary
and many-sided the resources of the Spirit are if we are to reach
mature humanity, "to the measure of the stature of the fullness of
Christ."[6] The way in which the Spirit works makes clear two aspects
of the nature of Christian maturity which are vital to the development
of this whole argument. The first is that this maturity is known only in
relationship. Our humanity is cohumanity. As 1 Corinthians 12 and
Ephesians 4 emphasize, the gifts of the Spirit are given to each only
for the sake of all, because it is together and not separately that those
who follow Christ achieve maturity. In this, the Pauline writings are
reflecting the teaching of the Bible as a whole. This unity in community is implied in the teaching of Jesus concerning the kingdom and, as
Barth has so extensively argued,[7] it is in this sense that Christians are
to understand the second creation story in Genesis.

Second, because maturity is discovered only in relationship, we
have a mutual interest in each other's growth toward maturity.
Spiritual gifts are provided for the building up of the body of Christ,
his instrument for expressing the service of God in the world. Without
this building up, we remain undeveloped, "children, tossed by the

waves and whirled about by every fresh gust of teaching, dupes of crafty rogues and their deceitful schemes.''[8] As we shall see more fully when we come to consider the church as a school of maturity, the Christian community is meant to be the place where, above all others, fellow members of Christ neither keep each other down nor put each other down but build each other up, as the necessary condition of growth toward a common maturity.

Because it possesses this communal character, the liberation that Christian maturity brings has always to be expressed in specific terms. We are not released into an abstract freedom, like prisoners who suddenly find themselves outside the prison gate one cold morning with nothing to do, nowhere to go, and no one to meet them. Nor are we left simply to celebrate and stay with, constantly trying to relive the experience of liberation itself. This is what romanticism supposes, whether in religious or secular guise, and it is a supposition which is again having one of its frequent revivals. As Barth emphasizes in his great discussion of freedom in *Church Dogmatics* IV.3, one is released only to discover one's vocation, and it is always a vocation that has reference to the community. The recovery of freedom means the recovery of the power of choice, and choice, once made, inevitably carries with it limitation. One goes here and not there, does this and not that. The calling is for a particular purpose and any gifts which are received are intended to help with the fulfillment of that purpose. What is more, not only does choice involve limitation but limitations are imposed on the range of options open to one because of the nature of one's calling. Freedom is freedom for one's neighbor, the release from self-preoccupation to be available for one's neighbor, to become a ''man for others.'' It is the neighbor's needs, and the positive possibilities of constructive action which open up in association with the neighbor, which condition the nature of the choice.

''Permissiveness,'' as it is called today, or ''license,'' as it used to be called, is the irresponsibly selfish attempt to break out from the pattern of mutual obligation in which freedom alone has any meaning. This employs the excuse that, as always happens in life, some older patterns of meaning have become unnecessarily restrictive and need to be looked at afresh. In Pauline terms, such an attitude is not one of freedom but of enslavement, and enslavement not to the law but to what he means by the flesh, arbitrarily self-centered existence. Even when the individual's vocation may demand a creative breakthrough into the unknown which has to be taken alone and when it may seem to go against the will of most of his or her fellows, as such breakthroughs often do, it will still have reference to the community. Only God can call anyone to such a vocation, and the Lord's Prayer explicitly warns us to pray that we may be spared such a test. To take it upon oneself, casting off the support of the community, is to tempt God. Part of the meaning of the cross is that Jesus has now gone before us to endure that particular trial alone. Those who demand in their pride, like Thomas, to see Jesus' hands and side before being prepared to receive his peace, commission, and Spirit, show that they are not to be trusted with that isolation.

The more fully the liberation of the Christian works out in practice, the more it expresses itself in identification with one's neighbor and in the overcoming of alienation both from the neighbor and from the place in which one has been placed in life as a result of one's vocation. The notion of alienation has usually been discussed with reference to the Marxist analysis of the relation between the worker and his or her skill or, more recently, to what constitutes mental health, but in Christian terms, it refers primarily to our relation with God and, through God, with each other and the natural order. What happens must not be oversimplified. On the one hand, anyone who has heard the call of Christ is made more acutely aware of alienation than he was before. As he comes to himself, it becomes clear to him how far he has strayed from his home, and how long the road back has to be. But he sees this only when he knows that the way back is now open, that his past failures have been forgiven, and that his father is ready to restore him. The last thing he will be tempted to do, therefore, is to take pride in being alienated, to tell stories of how excitingly tough life was among the swine when they shared their husks with him, and to contrast his past with the unadventurous dullness of the life of his stay-at-home elder brother.

The notion of identification has also been much discussed recently, often in the same context, but sometimes in as distorted a way as that of alienation. Everything depends on whom one identifies with and the way in which one does it. The mature Christian will realize that it is possible even to use an act of identification as a way of expressing covert alienation, a demonstration against someone who will disapprove of one's action rather than a genuine commitment to the one with whom one appears to be identifying oneself. This is why the rule has to be that true identification begins with one's nearest neighbors, those for whom one has the most direct responsibility. They are those, therefore, in relation to whom one is likely to feel most alienated, especially if they belong to a different age group, race, church, social class, or level of education from oneself.[9] It is with these persons that reconciliation is likely to be most difficult, most undramatic, and ultimately most rewarding. As Jesus said to the Syro-Phoenician woman in his semi-ironical conversation with her, his first vocation was to the house of Israel. He implied that it is only when one has managed to straighten out relations with those who are nearest that one has a basis from which to begin to have a genuinely helpful relation to those who are farther away. However, as she reminded him in the only incident in Scripture where Jesus is successfully answered in kind, they also may have a claim on one's attention.[10] In relations between Christians and Jews this is still an unresolved, and inexcusably neglected, issue. Its meaning for social and political priorities has to be determined by each Christian individual and group in its own situation.[11]

The communal nature of Christian liberation, and the fact that we need all the gifts of the Spirit granted to the community if we are not again to be led astray, also throws light on the relation between the strength that seems to come directly from Christ in the Spirit and what appears to be ordinary human strength. The latter implies the capacity to handle oneself and one's relation with one's neighbor and with the world around oneself in ways which compel the respect of the Christian believer when he or she looks out on the world from his or her own point of view. There is obviously a great deal of strength in the world that does not seem to stem directly from Christian inspiration. What its origins are, and what its relation is to the exclusive Christian claim to salvation, are important questions which cannot concern us here. Two points are relevant to this argument. The first is that, insofar as this is genuine strength and not a proud attempt at self-sufficiency or dominance, the mature Christian is glad to find it and welcome it as an added resource to what he already knows through the Spirit. As Bonhoeffer came to see so clearly, nothing is more base than for the Christian to suppose that the honor of his or her faith demands that he or she disparage such strength and seek to undermine it because it did not originate within the Christian community. The success of the disciples of the crucified Christ may be very different from success as the world normally understands it, but there are some forms of success to be found in the world that survive the crucified Christ's test and, when they do, we can be sure that they receive his blessing. Fortunately for us, God has dealings with humankind independent of professional Christians.[12] By the same token, however, the other point also holds. Such strength is at least as vulnerable as any more directly generated within the Christian community. The so-called secular rich man will not find it any easier to enter the kingdom than the religious rich man. Our faith should train us to detect the kind of strength we find in Christ wherever it appears in the world, and then so identify ourselves with those who possess it that we can share with them, in the ways most acceptable to them, the resources we possess from Christ to help make the most of that strength and overcome the difficulties which it creates.

The fact that Christ came not to call the righteous but sinners to repentance does not contradict the truth of this. His words were addressed ironically to those whom the world calls righteous, those who are as strong as humankind knows strength, and the implication is that their very strength should make them see his point. They, above all people, should be able to understand why he set about his mission in the way he did, since their very strength should make them realize their vulnerability and their need for grace. It is they who see most clearly that the kingdom can only be entered by those who have become as little children. For example, there is an element of humbug in protestations of humility on the part of those who are weak. As the saying is, they so obviously have so many things to be humble about that there is no need for them to call attention to the fact. When they do so, it is hard to avoid the suspicion that they are doing so either out of self-pity or in order to gain a hidden advantage over the strong by making them feel guilty. The qualities displayed by maturity in weakness are not so much those of humility as those of patience, courage, and independence of spirit. It is very hard for human beings to be honestly humble, and it is most likely to arise when, in freedom, we fulfill our vocation to the limit of our capacity and have to confess that, having done all, we remain unprofitable servants.[13] Thus, it is generally those who achieve most, especially in the arts and sciences, who are often the most unaffectedly humble, because the more they penetrate the mystery of existence, the more they realize how much there is still to discover and how much they depend on insights that come from beyond themselves if they are to find any of it.

Because his task was so great, Jesus was able to see it unreservedly in terms of service, and this is why his example of humility carries so much conviction. He did not consider it a prize to be greedily snatched at to be on an equality with God.[14] As we might say, he was so sure of his status and had such a tremendous work to do, that he was free to take the form of a bondslave and there to suffer humiliation and death. Those who possess the power, the *exousia,* of Christ should be able to do the same.

Apart from anything else, it is only when people start from this position of assured strength that they can presume to undertake the hazardous, and possibly invidious, role of being the servants of their fellows. We are told to fear the Greeks when they come bearing gifts but the same is true of all gift bearers, and Christians are no exceptions. Indeed, the greater the gift, the greater the danger, for giver and receiver. Even if the service is itself free from servility, the gift can easily encourage servility in those at the receiving end if the terms of the gift are not properly made clear. However genuinely the Christian may set out only to serve, the service itself can quickly become a justifying work that leads him or her to develop a vested interest in having a suitable number of servees in a dependent relation. The fact that this happens with groups no less than with individuals, as the history of many service agencies in society makes all too clear, only complicates the matter further. This is why it matters that Christians should see both that the impulse to serve should arise from strength and that its concern should be the restoration or the evocation of strength. The service is successful only when it is rendered without losing the respect of the one served and when his or her self-respect and power of independent action are built up in the process.[15]

The classical Reformed teaching about justification by faith is particularly helpful at this very point because it insists that the root of the impulse to serve others lies, not in the desire to justify ourselves, but in gratitude to God for the way in which we ourselves have been helped. That gratitude in its turn is made sincere and humble because it knows that we were helped in a situation where we were quite unable to help ourselves. The parable that is commonly taken as the most clear directive to Christian service is that of the Good Samaritan, but it teaches a falsely patronizing idea of service if we identify ourselves, as most of us are disposed to do, too readily with the Samaritan, usually forgetting his disreputable "outsider" status as we do so. Jesus asked the lawyer who put the original self-justifying question to place himself in the situation of the man who fell among thieves, where he was grateful for any help given without questions asked and where he could do nothing in return. We shall miss the force of the parable unless we try to do the same. It is grace apprehended on this level that alone produces authentic Christian service and it is only as we strive to continue to conform all our activities to this grace, even after our service has evoked gratitude in its turn, that we can express the liberation that is in Christ and grow toward mature humanity.

2

The Qualities of
Christian Maturity

THE NEW TESTAMENT, as we have said, is a success story. Even the
Passion narrative, Karl Barth has argued, is misread unless it is
placed firmly within the setting of a celebration of the royal majesty of
Christ.[1] The narrative makes clear the nature of the new life which is
open to humankind through Jesus Christ, as the realization of mature
humanity, while at the same time revealing the radical terms on which
alone it can be enjoyed. This is the central theme of the whole New
Testament, but it is stated most directly in terms of the particular
interest of this book in the Sermon on the Mount and in some of the
brief ethical exhortations to be found in Paul's letters. Our exposition
will chiefly rely on these.

In considering first some passages from the Sermon on the Mount,
we must remind ourselves again that it is addressed to members of the
new Israel, who abound in the riches and strength of the heirs of an
eternal covenant. This may not be immediately obvious because the
Sermon opens with references to the blessedness of those who are
poor in spirit and who suffer poverty and persecution in this life.
These are solemn warnings that Christian success is very different
from success according to the world's reckoning and that it always
carries with it a share in the burden Christ bore. In their own place,
these warnings will always demand the most serious attention from all
Christians. What is significant for our present purpose, however, is
the speed with which the mood changes to a more positive, it might
almost be called a more light-hearted one, which remains dominant
throughout the rest of the Sermon. Unless this is seen it is hard to
make sense of some of the most familiar passages, yet they make

11

complete sense when it is. The result of failure to see this positive mood has been a great deal of anxiety and misplaced heroics on the part of many Christians who, with unimaginative literalness, take as austere moral demands passages which are meant to be liberating and joyful.

This can be illustrated first by reference to one of the Beatitudes themselves: "Blessed are the meek, for they shall inherit the earth." Meekness is taken today to be a quality of the weak. The meek are the passive, the spineless, those born to be put upon, nature's doormats. How could the likes of them inherit the earth, and why indeed should they? The inclination of the meek is always to retreat from power, and they would not know what to do with the earth if they did inherit it. The most they could do would be to discover some perverse strength fired by resentment, the worm turning, rarely an effective and never an attractive quality, well worthy of the contempt poured on it by Nietzsche. But this, of course, is not what the passage means at all, any more than it is what similar passages in the Magnificat mean. "Meekness" in the seventeenth century was a quality of strength and the word used is now better translated, as the New English Bible does, "those of gentle spirit." An appropriate picture to have in interpreting this Beatitude is that of the gentle giant, a large heavy athlete, who wants to win the confidence and inspire the affection and obtain the cooperation of a timid little boy. He lowers his voice and carefully controls his cumbersome movements, perhaps even getting down on his knees, so that he can allay the boy's fears and make it easy to communicate with him. When he can make the boy see that his strength is under the control of his gentle will and that all he wants to do is to help and enjoy the boy's company, then the strength becomes a reassurance rather than a threat. The child becomes the stronger because of it and a constructive relationship is now possible.

It is very significant for understanding what Christian obedience means in terms of politics and public affairs at the present time that this Beatitude should be placed in immediate conjunction with one which praises those who hunger and thirst after righteousness, or that the right should prevail. Those who are themselves liberated rightly desire to help others find liberation, initially that fundamental liberation which Christ brings but one that also has repercussions for liberation from oppression on all the levels of ordinary life in the world. This will give them a passion that the right will prevail, a passion that is likely to intensify as they find that their new life endows them with the insight, courage, and perseverence which bring success. This passion, it is important to note, Jesus calls a blessing to those who possess it and it will bring results. The right will prevail. Yet, like other blessings, it has its dangers. Nothing is easier than to overwhelm even those we wish to help with our own zeal. In the process, they may be forced to conform to our interpretation of what their liberation should mean and lose sight of their own vocation, as those who are answerable to God in their own right. In the end, if no limit is set to our passion, all that will happen is that they exchange one servitude for another, with the added tribulation that they are expected to show gratitude to their new conquerors for delivering them from their former masters.

This is why it matters that those who have a zeal for righteousness should also be those of gentle spirit. This is true in directly personal relationships and no less true in political, and especially international, affairs. Only those who have transcended themselves sufficiently to have a gentle spirit can be trusted to have their hunger and thirst that the right should prevail satisfied; they realize that the right is not simply their own possession and that liberation for others means having room for discovering their own vocation without interference even by their liberators. It is also being brought home to us with increasing force today that this has application not only to human relations but also to the relation of humanity as a whole to the natural order. If humankind refuses to deal with nature in a gentle spirit but arrogantly rips out its secrets and plunders it to satisfy humankind's every unconsidered whim, on the assumption that this is automatically righteous, its dominion over nature will be taken away and it will find that it no longer inherits the earth.

The other Beatitude which singles out a particularly significant quality of Christian maturity is that which says, "Blessed are the peacemakers, for they shall be called the children of God," for the making of peace is integral to growth into full maturity. Peace, in Augustine's phrase, is the tranquillity of order but the Bible would not understand this in the static, hierarchical sense it has sometimes held in the course of Christian history. It is that unity of heart and mind which enables us to work and grow together, the peace of an ideal family which the Spirit-sustained church is meant to enjoy, conveyed by the great biblical word, *shalom*. The New Testament sees the world left to itself as always in process of slipping back into that primeval chaos, that radical disorder, where there is no meaning and no significant purpose, out of which it was originally called by God. When people are at odds with each other, they are caught up in that process. In such situations, the limitation, or preferably the halting of their hostilities, may initially be the only thing to be done, but no one should be under any illusion that that in itself constitutes the making of peace. As Jacques Ellul has reminded us in his study of violence,[2] the letting loose of brute force to have its own way is not patient of Christian resolution. Peace becomes a possibility only when the violence stops and people are able to treat each other as human beings again, to listen to each other, to adjust their attitudes to each other, and to build up sufficient confidence in each other to make and hope to keep agreements. This is why, as again Ellul points out, a great deal of Christian peacemaking has to be quiet and unspectacular. Even trying to mediate between conflicting groups and individuals, which Christians will often be led to do, is only a second best, an attempt to make up for earlier failures in true peacemaking. A mature understanding of what making peace involves will lead Christians to be farsighted, sensitive, and vigilant, always looking well ahead and having efficient early warning systems about where breakdowns in relationship might occur and violent conflict ensue and always ready to move in quickly before all communication breaks down. Violent conflict is sometimes inevitable but when it occurs it is an occasion for penitence for all concerned. When it is brought to an end, the result cannot in itself be a victory in any sense which Christians can recognize, however much they may welcome it if they support what appears to be the winning side. It is no more than the end of a damaging emergency, like the putting out of a fire. The possibility of a victory for righteousness only arises when the terms of the new relationship that emerges from the conflict are considered. Do they make for the building of peace?

All this should be obvious enough in a Christian context but it is disturbing that it should be lost sight of in some of the romanticization of violence which takes place in Christian circles today, often curiously claiming that this is a particularly radical form of Christianity in doing so. It is true that in one very radical sense Jesus brought not peace but a sword, but it was the sword of God's word, dividing between the joints and the marrow of the heart's intents. It was no club with which to batter the outsides of people into physical submission. The Christian life is a matter of conflict with evil, and issues have to be faced and sometimes they have to be forced. Christians themselves may disagree and have to go their separate ways. That happened, we are told, even with Paul and Barnabas, and Barnabas was "a good man, full of the Holy Ghost and of faith." Nor can Christians stand aside when the clash of conflicting powers is involved, even when the power involves the use of violence. Situations may arise when they have to become "freedom fighters," or when they may think it right to support "freedom fighters." Yet all the time they will not lose sight of the fact that, however close the relation may be between the two in some contexts, that freedom is never the same as the freedom already given in Christ, a freedom that gives them a distinctive expertise in making peace rather than war. Christian radicalism does not prompt us to go out into the world with chips on our shoulders, spoiling for a fight, but enables us to look for the root of the difficulty in a troubled situation to see whether it can be removed. Knowing the importance of self-criticism, especially when one is consumed by a zeal for righteousness, we should be able to see possibilities of communication and fresh understanding in situations of conflict and have patience to work for their realization. We will know how intractable human nature is, especially in its self-justifying moods, and we will expect the work of making peace to be slow and difficult, allowing for setbacks without discouragement. We will also know that when peace in a particular situation is achieved, it will remain precarious. We will not be surprised when a new threat emerges, because there is no abiding peace on earth. Yet we will persevere, because the making of peace, which reflects the enduring divine order in the midst of the broken fragments of human orders, remains the most rewarding of all human activities.

When peacemaking is looked at in this way, a totally different set of priorities from that which prevails among the most politically "militant" groups in society will then become established among Christians. More attention will be paid to strengthening positions of health and stability and to avoiding the complacency which erodes that health and stability than to those situations of crisis and breakdown which inevitably capture the headlines and invite spectacular action. In a world where many people are only too ready to blow up their neighbors and sometimes themselves, in order to prove that their cause is alone the righteous one, Christians will have the maturity to cultivate the arts of diplomacy, thoughtfulness, coolness, and unwearying patience and give their strongest moral support to those who, whether they bear a Christian name or not, display those qualities in human affairs. These are the keepers of peace, who make possible the activities of the makers of peace.

The third quality of maturity is generosity. Some of the most familiar passages in the Sermon on the Mount provide examples of how this quality is to be exercised. I refer particularly to turning the other cheek, giving one's shirt as well as one's coat and walking the second mile, and also to the warnings against anxiety about food, drink, and clothing. The whole spirit of these passages is lost if they are taken as calls to heroic self-sacrifice. They are put forward cheerfully, one might almost say in an offhand way, as though Jesus is not expecting his followers to find what he is saying either surprising or difficult to put into practice. These are words spoken to the rich, who are being told to behave with the confident style and openhanded generosity appropriate to their status and their great expectations. When they are told to turn the other cheek, it is misleading to have a picture of someone suffering a rain of blows with drawn face and an air of martyrdom. It is true that Christians who follow their Lord will sometimes be called to suffer in exactly that way, taking onto themselves all the weight of the evil in a particular situation, so that it dies there and is carried no further. The last of the Beatitudes emphasizes and reiterates this[3] and, coming immediately after the Beatitude on peacemaking, suggests that peacemakers may well find that such persecution will often be part of their lot. But this is surely not where the emphasis lies in these particular passages. For example, in turning the other cheek, I think again of the gentle giant, perhaps a big, good-humored, craggy boxer, against whom a small boy is testing his strength. When the boy hits him as hard as he can on one side of the face, he laughs and turns the other cheek, saying, "Come on, hit harder. See if you can hurt me this time." Jesus is reminding his hearers that, with the resources of their strength, they can afford to be generous.

Similarly, the warnings about anxiety at the end of the sixth chapter of Matthew are not a call either to heroic austerity or to that kind of anxiety that is sometimes called "living by faith," where people serving a good cause spend so much time praying for the check mysteriously to drop through the letter box at the last minute that their very prayer becomes a form of worry. Jesus is saying that worry is the congenital vice of the rich, and that it is basely and stupidly unnecessary. What have they got to worry about? They have plenty. If even the lilies of the field are taken care of, surely the heirs of the kingdom can take their economic problems in their stride and not have to spend time and energy in bothering about them. They literally have better things to think about. To seek God's kingdom and his righteousness will produce the creative unrest which generates sufficient energy to allow them to organize their temporal affairs without difficulty. They will have that detachment in relation to everyday things and that assurance concerning God's goodness that will give them the margin which enables them to be generous.

In their freedom from worry, the heirs of the kingdom have the will as well as the means to be generous. Here what has already been said about gratitude as the impulse to service becomes important. Gratitude makes one want to share what one has received with others, not merely because it is right but because one needs the others to join in the celebration and add to the delight. Gratitude overflowing in delight is irresistible. When Christians come bearing gifts in this spirit, there is no need to fear them because all hint of patronage is removed and equality is confirmed. All are enriched and all grow in stature. Nothing is further from the spirit of the Sermon on the Mount than the censorious meanness of the rich who, having put their trust in riches, become obsessed with anxiety about their safety, doling out even their charity with strings carefully attached and sensing potential subversion behind every begging bowl. This is not to say that giving can be thoughtless. In our last section we shall have to consider why to give well has to be treated as an art, which needs more cultivation than it normally receives. What is essential is that the spirit in which one gives should express the life-enhancing generosity appropriate to the way in which one has received.

For the fourth quality of maturity we turn to the Letter to the Philippians where, warning his readers against anxiety in the same way as the Sermon on the Mount does, Paul says in a concluding exhortation, "Let your *epieikēs* be manifest to all."[4] The elusiveness of this quality of *epieikēia* is indicated by the difficulties which the translators have had with it. It has been variously rendered "moderation," "tolerance," "forbearance," and as in the New English Bible and perhaps best of all, "magnanimity."[5] Each of these lights up a different aspect, but magnanimity may be best because it brings out the element of largeness of spirit, reflecting the divine fullness and, as we have seen, expressing itself in generosity, which is central to the notion of maturity. The context is significant. "Rejoice in the Lord always, again I say, rejoice. Let your magnanimity be manifest to all. The Lord is near. Have no anxiety but in everything make your requests known to God in prayer and petition with thanksgiving. And the peace of God which passes understanding will keep guard over your heart and your thoughts in Christ Jesus." It is important not to miss the eschatological reference. He is saying: "You know Christ's victorious power and rejoice in it. He is at hand. The final resolution of all things is imminent. In all this, you possess already that peace, that inward harmony, which nothing in the world can destroy because it comes from God and is protected by Christ himself. This is why you can show magnanimity. You recognize that all your actions and judgments have to be provisional. You could be wrong and your neighbor could be wrong but you need not worry unduly about this. The Lord, with whom you are in contact and who knows your situation, will set it right when he comes and his will is one of grace and forgiveness. Even if your neighbor *is* wrong, therefore, and especially if he has offended you, you do not need to be too officious in setting him right. Since he is so near at hand, you are free to anticipate the Lord's forgiveness. And anyway, you know that nothing that any wrongdoer does can violate the peace in your heart and your thoughts over which Christ stands guard. In your strength, you can afford to be magnanimous, tolerant, forbearing, free from a fanatical zeal for righteousness, moderate."

It hardly needs to be underlined how important this quality is in a time when passions are aroused and people are filled with a zeal for righteousness which lacks gentleness of spirit and generosity, making them more concerned that their own conception of what is right should prevail than that it should make for peace. It provides a justification for Christian support of what are sometimes called "moderate" or "liberal" policies, particularly in the political sphere where matters that are essentially relative can easily be absolutized. To say this, however, is not to offer a euphemism for mere mediocrity, which never knows when to make a stand or to sharpen an issue when the situation demands it. Reinhold Niebuhr demonstrated in ways which have been forgotten with depressing rapidity in some sections of the Christian community that "moderate" and "liberal" policies in the kind of social democracy in which such policies must readily prevail are a mark not of timidity and the refusal to face the responsibilities of power but of a high maturity and a realistic appraisal both of the potentialities and the dangers of political action.[6] This maturity is magnanimous and forbearing as well as moderate, concerned to look beyond a particular conflict to seek a basis on which peace can be built, because its eschatological perspective enables it to see farther than the eyes of those who are concerned only with what they conceive to be justice now, and on their own terms. It is not swayed by the adolescent temptation to absolutize its own insights and then to lose patience and seek an outlet for its frustrations in violence when things do not work out exactly as it expected. It is this magnanimity, much more than the power of government so much emphasized by traditionalist theologians as a dike against sin, which helps to preserve the world unto the day of judgment, and it does so, as the apostle implies, through anticipating the nature of that merciful judgment by the way in which it handles power here and now.

The fact that it arises in the context of eschatological expectation is what makes this quality of *epieikēia* so different from the lukewarmness and mediocrity with which it might easily be confused. That expectation does not encourage the deferment of decision but rather the intensification of experience.[7] Knowing that the Lord is near means that judgment is also near. The good and the evil are seen to be ripening together unto the day of judgment and, as the Gospels constantly insist, this gives urgency to decisions here and now. The goodness of the good and the evil of the evil stand out all the more clearly and the time is short in which to make clear where one stands. Yet all this takes place with the knowledge that the judgment is not ours but the Lord's and that we shall be judged along with our opponents, and judged after the manner of Christ's dealings when he was in the midst of humankind. This makes us vigilant and alert, delivering us from quietism as well as from fanaticism, making our action in the affairs of this life incisive and to the point and, because it is informed by charity, essentially constructive. As Karl Barth has shown so superbly in his long discussion of "Man in his Time,"[8] it gives us the ability to do the right thing at the right time and also the composure to be content to wait when waiting is the only thing left to do.

Because it is so forward-looking, it also enables us to be delivered from any temptation to seek revenge. We need not nurse resentment when we suffer a defeat, resentment which diminishes our own stature and undermines all hope of making peace, and we can afford to be magnanimous in victory. Liberation is prize enough and one wants to share it even with those who previously stood in the way of its achievement. In the light of the knowledge that the Lord is near, it is silly to behave like the new rich who take pleasure in looking down on those who previously looked down on them. We have the promise and the warning that when the Lord comes, such behavior will quickly meet its deserts.[9]

The eschatological perspective also gives the necessary detachment, the sense of holding oneself in, the forbearance, which is also an element of *epieikēia,* and which prevents us from being the prisoners of our own time. Such imprisonment means, as the New Testament would say, subjection to the powers of this present age. It safeguards the more impressionable among us against mere trendiness, which may give the illusion of progressive movement but which is, in fact, no more than being swayed from side to side, being "tossed to and fro by every gust of teaching," the opposite of growth toward maturity. Instead of panting after the spirit of the age, we press toward our own goal and this enables us to foresee things which are to come, after the manner of the prophets, and to be prepared to meet them.

Finally, maturity is joyful. "Rejoice in the Lord always, and again I say, rejoice." This is a theme which resounds through the whole New Testament, standing in the strongest contrast to the joylessness of much life today, vacillating as it does between the moody discontent of adolescence and the self-pitying cynicism of unhappy old age, a joylessness sometimes reflected in the internal life of the Christian community. It is a joy of anticipation of the glory to come, which is so great that it overflows into a zest for life here and now. It cannot wait until the new life "to be clothed upon with its habitation which is from above" and starts trying to live now as though it were already there, transforming its temporary resting places on this earth into the image of the homeland. The significance of this for the Christian attitude to play and to celebration of the Lord's day will be considered later. As Paul himself understood so well, this joy is always experienced in the midst of trouble,[10] yet when not having directly to put up with trouble,[11] the mature Christian should be filled with the strength which comes from joy, setting forth every morning, like the sun in the psalms, as a strong man to run a race.

More than that, as Paul goes on to remind his readers in the very next verses of the passage in Philippians which we have been discussing, this positive, confident attitude enables us to appreciate and make the most of all that we find good in the life of the world and the human heritage. We are to reflect on "whatsoever is true and noble and just and pure and loveable and gracious and excellent and admirable." In this one sentence, this Hebrew of the Hebrews shows his appreciation of the Greek ideal of *paideia* in its strength and, here without any hint of Christian imperialism, sees it as part of what faith can use for its upbuilding into maturity.[12] This should make Western Christians today ashamed that they do not make better use of and derive more enjoyment from all the privileges which they possess. Professional ministers must bear their share of the blame for this because they have not insisted sufficiently to the rich communities they serve that wealth without faith, including wealth produced as the fruit of faith, engenders anxiety, and anxiety provokes greed and the abuse of wealth, and the abuse of wealth creates envy and a spirit of emulation, which issue in ugliness and misery. It is small consolation to observe that the academic community may be even more to blame. Here, more than in its churches, society has poured its wealth since the war and it is here, above all, that life in the creation should be celebrated with delight; but it sometimes seems that here is where people have developed the greatest expertise in making themselves and each other unnecessarily miserable. One of the things which used to strike me most forcibly when I began to visit the USA from war-ravaged Europe, and which endeared the since much-abused

American way of life to most of the rest of the world, was the unaffected good humor of the people, as they honestly enjoyed life in a good place, a quality which shone through all the meretricious gloss even of old Hollywood films. One of the few justifications for the existence in their present form of the phenomenally prosperous suburban churches which are such a feature of the USA, and whose deficiencies as false abstractions from the totality of the life of the community America's internal critics so faithfully castigate, has been that they are, at least, singularly happy communities. If they have done nothing else, they have helped to build up the world's poor stock of that surplus good temper, nervous energy, and material resource which have given some people strength, and the magnanimity which comes from strength, to help face and overcome the difficulties of less-privileged places.

3

The Temptations of Maturity

To SAY what was said about American life at the end of the last chapter is not, of course, to tell the whole story. In particular, it should be carefully noted that this everyday cheerfulness is part of the overflow of Christian maturity rather than the expression of what lies at its heart. Perhaps it is an American heresy, reflected in the bland, eversmiling countenance of some of its sects, to place it at the heart. Yet provided Americans realize, as some of those who coined the phrases may not have done, that a country must have its roots very deep in grace before its members can see it as actually "self-evident" that people have "an inalienable right" to the "pursuit of happiness," they have cause for celebration that they belong to such a country.

This is the kind of proviso which the joyful pages of the New Testament seem always to be making. The richer we are, the more cause for celebration we have, the more vulnerable we become. The higher we rise, the further we fall. Lucifer was one of the greatest of the angels and, we are told, "from dawn to dewey eve he fell, a summer's day." Indeed, the temptations of maturity are more deadly than those of childhood and adolescence and, with growing maturity, vigilance must increase and not be relaxed. Again, it is noteworthy that the Letter to the Ephesians, which develops so richly the way in which the spirit of Christ enables us to realize the fullness of humanity in a cosmic setting, has to end with an appeal to put on the whole armor that God provides if we are to stand firm in our exalted position against all the onslaughts of the devil. To the extent that we grow into the fullness of the stature of Christ, we make a very large target. This is why a discussion of the qualities of maturity has to be followed immediately by a reminder of its temptations.

The first of these arises directly out of the new-found strength which liberation engenders. To the outward eye, as one human being among others, no one is more autonomous, more "inner-directed" and independent of external authority than the person who possesses faith. He is the veritable master of his fate and captain of his soul. Paul is Christ's bondservant but, as he frequently has to remind the obstreperous Corinthians, that does not mean that he is anyone else's bondservant except when Christ commands him to be, and the authority he possesses from Christ is not to be overridden. He was acutely aware, however, of the dangers of this position and, as his tortured convolutions in the Second Letter to the Corinthians so movingly reveal, he is at pains to avoid appearing to "boast" because of this. It is said of Calvin that he feared God always but man never. That is the authentic independence of Christian maturity, and it is a quality in short supply in the nervous Christian community today. The trouble is that such attitudes give those who possess them a great deal of power. When they find that their fearlessness leads others to go in fear of them, it is hard to remember that they are meant to be of gentle spirit and easy to exploit the situation in order to dictate to others what they should do for their own good. From this it is a short step to conclude that one is a strong person in one's own right, who does not need to fear God either, and to congratulate oneself on one's own unconquerable soul.

The sin of pride is a familiar enough theme of Christian moralists[1] but it has not always been seen how much it is a sin of advanced maturity and, therefore, how extremely subtle and insidious its operations are. Modern theology, aided by some elements in existentialist psychology, has exposed the way in which one can succumb to the pride of reason by showing that the range of experience within which one can be trusted to use reason honestly is much more circumscribed than most forms of rationalism will admit. It has not been so alert in showing that spiritual pride can be even more damaging. The cruder forms of a "holier-than-thou" attitude are readily detectable, not least when they express themselves in that false humility already mentioned. What is harder to discern, and still harder for anyone else to point out to the culprit, is the pride which arises from a serious attempt to be faithful to a difficult vocation, especially when it is unpopular and misunderstood. All spiritual vocation is costly, and it makes demands on others closely involved as well as on the person called, but it is very easy for the one called to dramatize himself or herself as the only faithful one and to develop the attitudes of a superior person, especially when the others show signs of stumbling under the weight of the burden he or she has caused to be laid upon them.[2]

The line between dedication and self-importance is very fine, and the very devotion that successful leaders inspire can encourage them to cross it. Jesus had to face this danger in his third temptation and it is one reason why he is so emphatic that the true leader must take the form of a servant. The recognition of this is what distinguishes mature Christians from "charismatic" cult figures. They have nothing within them of the egotism of the romantic artist, who sacrifices others, especially members of the other sex, to his or her own conception of the exigencies of his or her genius, nor do they have the spirit of the tycoon, who incorporates the bones of his or her victims in monuments to his or her own glory. Yet they will also know how near at hand attitudes like these are, especially when they are confronted by the claims of rivals to spiritual authority. This is what makes Paul's insight in 2 Corinthians so remarkable, when he has to assert his apostolic authority and resist attempts to undermine it while at the same time trying to avoid self-aggrandizement and to retain the basis for making peace with those who are attacking him.

Paul is hardly less aware of the next danger, which arises from pride, and that is complacency. He shows this in his bitterly sarcastic contrast, in the fourth chapter of the first letter to them, between the Corinthian *phronimoi*, the wiseacres, "such successful Christians" as the New English Bible calls them, and the apostles themselves, who are like the scum of the earth. Again, it is necessary to see how it is success itself which breeds complacency, and success which is the fruit of genuine faith. If one has ventured into the unknown, risking all in the leap of faith, floating on seventy thousand fathoms, and finds one's faith vindicated, what then? Having first sought God's kingdom and his righteousness, in due season one finds that the good things of this life also are added unto one. It would be pusillanimous and ungrateful not to enjoy them but it quickly becomes the easiest thing in the world to assume that they are one's natural birthright and that nothing more is required than to go on enjoying them.

No one has described more vividly the radicalism of the leap of faith than Søren Kierkegaard in his book *Fear and Trembling*,[3] as he reflects upon the significance of the Genesis story of Abraham and God's demand that he sacrifice his son Isaac. However, he does not face the question of what happens after Isaac has been handed back to Abraham and the old man is faced with all the problems of the boy's upbringing. The difficulties he would have had to deal with would have been more complex, if not more intense, than those that confronted him in his test, both because Isaac would seem even more precious to him after the immense agony of having to raise the knife to kill him and because it would seem to be only reasonable that he was now free simply to enjoy his son in his own old age. Yet the later history of Israel stands to make clear that this would have been insufficient.

This infinitely rich story suggests another way in which complacency frequently creeps in, a way which is a warning against the trivialization of spiritual temptation. This trivialization can easily lead those who consider themselves to be spiritually "serious" to assume that, because they are not likely to succumb to it in its obvious forms, therefore this, at least, must be a temptation from which they can claim immunity. Suppose Isaac, in his turn, becomes aware of the cost at which his life has been won, and now understanding both the greatness of his father's love toward himself and his greater love for God, realizes how infinitely precious his heritage is and how heavy a responsibility he has to maintain it. In the most admirable way Isaac becomes a conservative, because it is possible even to become a conservative guardian of the radicalism of faith—forgetting, as we all do, that no one has the courage to be genuinely radical except in an existential situation where, like Abraham, he is left with no alternative. The more Isaac finds others to be ignorant of the meaning of that heritage, perhaps even so completely missing the point as to denounce his father as the murderer of his own child, the more determinedly defensive he is driven to be. But this inexorably means that he becomes more interested in his past than in his future. The powerful influence of religious nostalgia begins its work, nostalgia which is all the more powerful the greater the radicalism of faith out of which the heritage was created. This means that his horizons begin to contract and what lies ahead, with all the changes it will bring, seems increasingly threatening. He forgets that the fulfillment of the promise to his father still lies in the future and that he has his own part to play, on the same terms, in its realization. He ceases to be a pilgrim and becomes content to remain where he is, making the most of what he has, and the thought of raising the knife to kill his own children makes him recoil with horror. Thus complacency is born, at the very point where the fruit of living faith is being gathered. The implication of this for the church's self-understanding is obvious.

The next step in the progression away from living faith is sloth. Karl Barth, in volumes IV.1 and IV.2 respectively of his *Church Dogmatics,* has two long chapters on the pride and the sloth of humankind, and there is an obvious connection between the two. Those of his critics who argue that he exalts the function of the theologian unduly might be disposed to hint that he has not escaped the first sin but even the sternest of them, contemplating the vast scope and size of *Church Dogmatics* could hardly charge him with the other, so that his words on the subject have extra authority. He analyzes sloth under the headings of stupidity, and that indifference to one's neighbor which issues in inhumanity, of the dissipation which is the sign of loss of control, and of the worry which arises because one knows that one is failing to fulfill one's vocation and lacks the energy to do anything about it. He produces a series of vivid Old Testament examples of these different aspects of sloth which make excellent starting points for pastoral sermons on the subject. He also brings out what we have seen to be true in relation to pride and complacency, that these are often corruptions of virtues and can sometimes masquerade as such. Thus he argues, a little surprisingly, that sloth can hide itself behind an appearance of worldly wisdom. Barth particularly emphasizes, as one might expect, that Christians on the road to maturity are active people, pilgrims, who are concerned to keep moving toward their destination. Spiritual food is given them to sustain them on the journey, manna in the wilderness, sufficient for one day in one place. If, however, through pride and complacency, they become content to stay where they are, they begin to fall out of condition and to lose their appetite. The prospect of moving becomes increasingly unattractive and they use their energy chiefly to find excuses for inactivity, concentrating much more on the delights of the flesh than on the food of the spirit, and yet the prey of futile worry because they know that these are not enough to satisfy them. This is what leads, although Barth does not mention it at this particular point in his discussion, to the restless search for novelty, as a distraction, a way of passing the time when they have lost the preoccupations of the journey. This is the characteristic vice of old and tired civilizations, of cities which have become secularized wastelands as they have cut themselves off from the sources of renewal.

If, in a broad generalization, worry—with its concomitant of neurosis—might be described as the characteristic northern and Protestant consequence of sloth, then passivity—the listless, unreflective repetition of routine—is the characteristic southern, Catholic, and Orthodox consequence of sloth. This latter is an even more advanced form of retreat from Christian maturity.[4] It is important that in both its forms this sloth be recognized for what it is, so that its causes, rather than merely its symptoms, should receive treatment. There may, for example, be no point in continuing to do what earnest practitioners have been trying to do for a long time, to pump more and more spiritual food into those who suffer from sloth in the hope that they can be stirred into action. If they can no longer digest it or burn it up in creative energy, it will only make them fatter and slower than they were before, using even the masterpieces of the Christian past as mere distractions, switching them on and off between yawns. How best to deal with this situation is a matter for discussion. A period of enforced starvation, which compels them again to see the value of what they had taken for granted, may be the only way out for many. But even that does not always produce the desired result, and to try to bring it about, when we are surrounded by such riches that could be of great benefit to us if they were properly used, is a tempting of God. In a situation like this, it is essential that the Christian community should see that its shape in the world is meant to be determined by the way in which it tries to express the qualities of maturity and to avoid the vices of pride, complacency, and sloth which can easily arise as defects of those qualities, so that its members can continue to keep moving toward their goal.

4

Moving Out Into the World

THE RISEN Lord's commission to the apostles was to preach the gospel to the whole of creation, and therefore faithfulness to the gospel demands that the Christian community should always be moving out into a wider world, losing its self-preoccupation and sometimes even its self-consciousness in service to humankind. Earnest Christians, especially those inspired by the ecumenical movement, have rightly continued to say to each other for the last generation that ministry is properly fulfilled only in mission; but they have not found it easy to express their mission in any other terms than those of increasing the size and institutional stability of church organizations themselves. They have found much internal resistance when they tried to break out in new directions. It is the Spirit, not the churches as they have evolved over the years, that represents the first fruits of our eternal inheritance, and it is the Spirit, not the churches, that possesses power.

On the other hand, the task of the apostolic mission is to transform the world, not to serve it on its own terms for the fulfillment of its own goals and with its own weapons. Before he began his ministry Jesus himself had to clarify what this meant in his temptations, and this is the sharpest of reminders to his followers that at this point the dangers are particularly great. The dangers are certainly not weaker today than they have been in the past, and they are especially insidious in countries like Britain where Christian institutions have known considerable power in the past but now find their secular influence greatly diminished. The temptation becomes strong to join the race for secular power to make up for the loss of genuine spiritual power and to

29

pretend that one is really using spiritual power in doing so. Plausible arguments lie readily at hand in justifying this course. Courting those who possess political, economic, or social power may seem to be the way in which to regain influence over events and to keep the powerful in spiritual ways, thus proving the continuing "relevance" of the Christian faith. An even more attractive alternative is to identify oneself with those who aspire to wrest power from those who have it and who claim the righteousness of the powerless in doing so.

The trouble with this attitude is that it accepts the world too readily on its own terms.[1] The recently fashionable slogan that "the world must write the agenda for the church" overlooks the ambiguities involved in all relations between the Spirit, the church, the world, and the corruption inevitably created both by the exercise and by the loss of power. What those who use the slogan want to emphasize is, of course, true enough. The apostolic mission is directed to the world, and it is the needs of that world and not those of the church as a favored organization within the world that have to be met. The church is meant to be a saving remnant in the world and not a saved remnant out of the world. The Spirit is active in the world as well as in the churches, and sometimes its action can be more clearly discerned in the world than in the churches, occasionally even in opposition to the churches. All the same it is no less true that the forces which corrupt the church also corrupt the world. They probably do so all the more effectively because the countervailing forces are not so frequently invoked. Christian spokespersons need to be highly self-critical about the church, but they also need to be hypercritical about their attitude toward the world and the forces operative within it at those points where their mission impinges upon it.

When Christians try to do their part in meeting the world's needs, one of the first questions they have to ask is, "Who is drawing up the agenda for the world?" Admittedly it is the world's needs, not merely their own, that have to be met; but those needs have to be recognized and assessed in the light of Christ. When this is done, it may well turn out that they are different from those which the politicians, publicists, people of business, and the pressure groups who make most noise in the world say that they are. This is why it is not enough for Christians to say their prayers and read their Bibles and the newspapers in order to discover where their duty lies. The Bible itself has to be read theologically, that is, in its historical setting and according to disciplined Christian principles of interpretation; and the newspapers, even the so-called quality newspapers, have to be read with an acute awareness that their criteria of what constitutes news are only occasionally the same as the criteria of those whose first responsibility is to proclaim the good news. The servant of the Lord, we are told, "does not cry aloud, nor is his voice heard in the street," and the Lord did not speak to Elijah in the earthquake, wind, or storm but in the still, small voice which can be drowned in the roar of the presses and entirely missed by the inattentive. To echo yet another biblical metaphor, the seed of the kingdom, growing secretly, is unlikely to be visible even to the eyes of the keenest newshawk, still less to an impatient television camera, unless they have been put on the alert by the Spirit of Christ. Thus it is essential that Christians, as they move out into the world and become involved with its life, strive hard to maintain their distinctive independence of judgment.

Even in doing this, they will be careful not to dramatize themselves and claim too much for what they are doing. They are Christ's servants and are not in the same position as their master. Their task is smaller and more compassable. They will know that the world has already been overcome. Power has been made available to them through no merit of their own in order to help express the victorious power of Christ in the world. An element of proper detachment may, therefore, be present in their service to the world, as those who are in but not of it. They need not have any kind of chips on their shoulders; neither need they look officiously for opportunities to be rejected by the powerful in the world nor to curry favor with them. They have their own work to do and their own master to whom alone they are accountable. Jesus taught his disciples in the Lord's Prayer to say, "Spare us the test" ("deliver us from evil"), the kind of ordeal which made his own Spirit a battleground between the power of God and the forces of evil. His ministers can be grateful that, through his agony, bloody sweat, and death upon the cross, he has made it possible for them to be spared that test. They are able to call upon his strength without needing to prove anything to themselves or to anyone else, and this should release them to be modest and practical in trying to help their neighbors to serve God in the present.

This means that sober realism should be their guide in trying to define their function in the world that they are likely to find today. They should ask themselves what they are doing and how far they can honestly claim to be fulfilling the apostolic commission. To the extent that they cannot, by what right can they expect to be endowed with the power of the Spirit? Why should the Spirit's power be wasted by being poured out on little clergy or laity engaged for the most part in a predictable round of stylized activities? To suppose that it should be so used is to behave like Don Quixote, sallying forth to tilt at windmills and pretending to be dressed in the whole armor of God. Is not this the impression given by too many of the professional clergy, loaded down as they are not even with spiritual equipment but only with its outward forms—rituals, vestments, titles, and buildings—so heavy that they are often unable to move? In default of action, their temptation is to spend their time tending and polishing these forms until they become too weak for any real fighting.

Partly in legitimate protest against this attitude, many Christians today emphasize the importance of commitment as evidence of seriousness in the fulfillment of vocation. Here again, however, sober realism is necessary. This talk of commitment is particularly current among those who believe it right to take up a well-defined political attitude, often in cooperation with people who do not share their Christian beliefs, against opponents whose deeply deplored attitudes are described by the label of an "ism"—fascism, communism, racism, sexism, or even age-ism. Many of the opponents of the kingdom of Christ do indeed gather together under the banner of these "isms," but such an attitude on the part of Christians is a dangerous oversimplification. Their self-knowledge should make them aware that the world is too subtle, insidious, and pervasive to allow its presence to be made so obvious and external in that way. The existence of an "ism" may often be one of the signs of the demons' activity, although church leaders do well to remember that the demons also readily fit into ecclesiastical dress and can appear as Catholicism, evangelicalism, liberalism, or even as Reformed Protestantism. The fact remains that the real home of the demons is in the darkest recesses of the human heart itself. Therefore, they cannot be forced out into the open and confronted by argument and political controversy and still less by violence—all such encounters quickly degenerate into competitions in self-righteousness—but only by what the New Testament calls prayer and fasting. That means the conscious and disciplined effort to conform ourselves to the vocation of Jesus and to see what we oppose in the light of the judgment and forgiveness that come through him. Attacking the "ism" and its conscious representatives directly is to attack one political power with another. In the rough and tumble of life this may often be unavoidable, but the Christian who tries to be faithful to the vocation of Christ should be under no illusion as to the inevitable ambiguity of what issues from such a conflict. It will rarely be an unqualified triumph of righteousness. Only when Christians manage to move behind the abstraction of the "ism" to the basic human condition to which the gospel speaks can they dare to invoke the power of the Holy Spirit.

The power of the Spirit is likely to be given only for a vocation which is genuinely based on that of Jesus and for a task which requires power, reflecting the dimensions of that vocation for its fulfillment. Thus it would seem likely that those who try to cope in a Christian way with the greatly enlarged "powers" that have been placed in our hands by the degree of mastery over physical nature, provided by modern science and technology, will recover the power of the Spirit more readily than those who repudiate or evade those powers. It can hardly be accidental that these powers were first released in the Western world. This world claimed to be Christendom; and it was the most dynamic, reformist elements in the Christian culture of the West which did most to discover these powers, even if sometimes in tension with established ecclesiastical authorities. From a Christian point of view, it is hard to see how these powers can be used for constructive rather than destructive purposes, unless they are dedicated to God's glory by those who call upon the powers of the age to come and who see themselves, in hope, as the heirs of the Messianic kingdom, for whom "the creation in its bondage waits."[2]

The Spirit blows where it lists, and seems to take delight in confounding even the most knowledgeable and perceptive of human forecasts. It can rekindle new power in small groups who have withdrawn from modern civilization and all its pressures, or even in the members of conventional churches leading conventional lives in conventional suburbs. The latter indeed are so much despised in some circles that they may begin to qualify as one of those elements chosen of God to bring to naught the things that are, that no flesh should glory in God's presence (1 Cor. 1:28f.). Nevertheless, our knowledge of what is involved in proclaiming the good news in all of creation will lead to the expectation that the Spirit is most likely to respond to those who are driven to places where they share in decisions that help to shape the future of large numbers of their fellows, and where finding the right way forward strains them to the very limit of their human capacity. Those who try to set bounds to the terrible destructive power of modern war, or who discipline and channel nuclear energy, or who discriminate carefully in the way they conduct scientific research into the means of producing human life, or who struggle to overcome the social and political obstacles of primary poverty, or who strive to create a major work of art in the thin soil of the modern Western world, are the kind of people who would seem to be most likely to discover that the Spirit still has power to grant grace beyond that which we have the right to expect or deserve.

This is not to say that the Spirit will be given only to those who are in positions of worldly importance, or only in obvious or dramatic forms. Not only will the Spirit often be given to the oppressed or to the imprisoned and to people in dealing with evils in their private lives, but even in the public sphere its action will follow its own logic, not that of the world. The power of the Spirit will rarely be detectable to those who lack Christian discrimination, and even they may not be able to detect it immediately. Just because it is genuinely creative, it is more likely to take time to mature, to work through individuals and small groups rather than through large organizations, and also to be completely uninterested in publicity. Renewal, as Jacques Ellul insists, is more likely to come from below than from above. Yet however quietly and unobtrusively we may expect renewal to take place, it is not likely to happen at all unless those who seek to fulfill the apostolic commission strive to take the measure of those "high things which are exalted against the knowledge of God" (2 Cor. 10:5) and to call upon the powers that God has placed in their hands in order to subdue them to the power of Christ.

5

The Inescapable Problems
of Power

THE USE of power is inescapable because power is an essential element in human affairs. A large part of what we call history and an even larger part of what we call politics deals with the struggle to possess power—its corruption and its responsible use. Societies that have not known upheavals connected with the exercise of power have either been those which have enjoyed brief periods of peaceful high civilization, or those which have been very simply organized in circumstances of great stability and isolation. It is hardly surprising that problems related to power should be so pervasive in the world today. This is a complex and rapidly changing world, with large concentrations of mobile and highly articulate people who have great powers placed in their hands. That this creates tensions is, in itself, not so much evidence of our world's instability and possible decadence as of its vitality.

This is obvious enough on the physical plane. There can never have been a time when the appetite for "energy" has been more voracious or when the search for it has been more intensely and ingeniously pursued. Oil is the most coveted of the world's sources of this energy at present, and its possession or the lack of it is of immense importance to the balance of political power. The so-called totalitarian political movements of this century, both fascist and communist, are consciously based on detailed analyses of economic, military, and political power and their interrelation, with a view to discovering the most effective ways of capturing, exploiting, and maintaining them. The blitzkrieg, an effort to concentrate the maximum amount of power in one decisive blow, became the characteristic method of achieving these aims.

The power element may not be so blatant in the attempts by nations in the power of other, stronger nations (the latter are often significantly called "the Great Powers") to achieve independence of them, but those attempts remain struggles for power nonetheless. This is true even when the claim is made that these are efforts to achieve liberation and that they are made in the name of democracy, defined as the right of one person to one vote. It is not accidental that democracy is often the first casualty of the successful outcome of such a struggle. Effective democracy of the kind that has slowly emerged in some of the old, established countries of Europe and in America and those closely related to them only exists when the ambiguities inherent in the struggle for power are recognized, and when allowance is made for them in political procedures.

Even the so-called conflict of the generations, which has been given a good deal of public attention in these countries in recent years, has largely been, in fact, a conflict of ideals about how people should live their lives. When it has been more than an outbreak of an infectious disease of adolescence, it has been a struggle for power between those who possess jobs, income, status, and the freedom to make and implement decisions, and those persons who lack all of these elements of power and would like to have them. The restlessness of so many elaborately educated young people in the most privileged parts of the Western world, who have been maintained in a state of virtual adolescence for too long, is probably due as much to the frustration of the appetite for power and the opportunities which it brings as to any other single factor.

If, then, power is so pervasive, does it not follow that those who lack power are insignificant? What attention do they merit, unless perhaps the notice of those who might someday possess power or who can be exploited in their weakness by the powerful in struggles with their rivals? It is a cliché that politics is about power, and I have implied that the same is largely true about many other spheres of life. If anyone lacks or surrenders power, why trouble ourselves about them at all?

It has to be agreed that for those who try to absolutize power, no issue arises. But even if power is pervasive, and therefore inescapable, one cannot say that it can ever be realistically absolutized. After all, power only has significance in the context of human relationships and, as that term itself suggests, power is thus bound to be affected by the relativity of such relationships. The relationship between those who possess power and those who do not needs to be faced; attempts to deal with it exclusively on the level of the exercise of naked power nearly always fail. This was demonstrated on a horrific scale by the Nazis in their "final solution" in dealing with the Jews, and also by other totalitarian regimes in trying to silence their opponents.

The issue of the exploitation of power has to be faced, and it is made more acute just because it is a characteristic temptation of those who possess power to exaggerate what they can do through its exercise. Power itself quickly becomes tyrannical. Unless this is understood, power can become tyrannical with those who would be shocked at the idea that they might ever seem to behave like tyrants, just as much as it becomes tyrannical with those whose exercise of power is more blatant. More than that, power can become tyrannical over those who wield it as well as over those whom they tyrannize. It does, of course, increase the number of possibilities open to the powerful as compared with others, but once their choice is made, the constraints imposed upon them can quickly make them power's slaves. So much is this the case that it is possible to argue that the larger the possibilities are which power provides, the greater is the danger of enslavement. This is becoming increasingly obvious in relation to the technical power that has done so much to create modern industrialized society. People quickly become the slaves of the machine they have invented to minister to their own convenience, and as the machines multiply and as the social organization they demand for their production and use becomes more elaborate, it becomes more difficult to break out and to establish what seems to be a simpler and more liberated situation. It may be possible for individuals or small groups of the like-minded to live without the internal combustion engine or mass-produced goods, but it appears quite impracticable for large-scale societies like modern nations. In his book, *The Technological Society*,[1] Jacques Ellul claims that it is wholly impossible. Whether that is so or not, it is undeniable that it requires exceptionally strong leadership—power of another sort which it is harder to come by—to enable a large-scale society to become the master and not the slave of the machines that its own power has brought into being. The force of this becomes most intense at the point where technical, industrial, military, and political powers unite. Here the destructive possibility of power, even when ostensibly exercised in the cause of righteousness, stands most starkly revealed. They that take the sword will indeed perish by the sword, and they will take many with them when that sword is powered by nuclear energy. Power must be disciplined if we are to survive. The difficulty is that the greater the power, the harder it is to discipline.

Nor is the situation substantially different when the more refined and even the more spiritual forms of power are considered, although their impact may be more subtle and insidious. To suppose that power realities exist only on those levels where they can be measured quantitatively is to diminish their importance. Not only does this tend to miss out on the "soft" forms of power, such as those of influence, convention, or tradition, but it also masks some of its deadliest temptations. Stalin's question, "How many divisions has the Pope?" may be pertinent when troops are ranged against each other on the battlefield; but, in terms of the social and political factors with which rulers have to deal, the forces of those who look to the Pope for guidance in significant areas of their experience are far from negligible, as those who hold power in the Polish state have had cause recently to know. Even on the field of battle itself, loyalty to the Pope, or to other representatives of nonmilitary causes, may affect the degree of resolution with which the troops fight.

It is in the interrelation of physical and spiritual power that most of the problems concerning the use of power arise. Quite apart from the obvious fact that the attitude which people have toward physical power often determines its use—whether good, bad, or indifferent—spiritual power is itself creative in releasing fresh physical power. The intellect does not exist in a vacuum. It needs to be inspired to penetrate the mystery of existence, to look in this direction rather than that, and to find strength to persevere when problems defy ready solution. Spiritual power does not exist in a vacuum either but, as it expresses itself, has consequences in other spheres. The charismatic individual may find the first inspiration in loneliness and may initially succeed in exercising power over only a small band of devoted followers. But as his or her influence spreads, it motivates others to gather together to form an institution and, if that succeeds, it creates rules and laws which may be sufficiently strong to be reinforced by physical sanctions. The most apparently unworldly bodies, of which churches are the most striking example, can develop in this way and gradually win so much support that they become major structures of power in their own right, wielding that power on other levels than those which their founders may have envisaged—economic, political, and even military as well as on the less palpable levels of moral authority. It has been observed that the possession of a major center of religious pilgrimage—a Rome, Jerusalem, or Mecca—is a more enduring economic asset than the possession of an oil field. And those who set out genuinely to first seek God's kingdom and his righteousness have often found, to their own embarrassment and to their children's worldly advantage, that a large number of other good things have indeed been added unto them, with all the complications that the possession of such riches involves. The experience of the first American missionary families to Hawaii, where the parents went out to do good and the children remained to do well, has plenty of parallels. Power of one kind or another is both the condition and the consequence of creative action, and the more creative the action, the more power it is likely to generate.

The fact that power works in this way makes inadequate a merely negative attitude toward the problems raised by its pervasiveness and the possibilities of corruption which its pervasiveness brings. In view of the ease with which misunderstanding arises in this contentious field, perhaps it should be emphasized that this does not imply that what is usually called a pacifist reaction to many exercises of power is necessarily wrong. It could be possible, for example, to agree with what has just been said about the pervasiveness and the potentially creative nature of power, and yet to be convinced that certain forms of power must be abjured because, no matter who holds them, the consequences of their possession are inevitably destructive. Many would argue that this is true of participation in the manufacture and use of massively destructive weapons of war, and others would argue the same in relation to the pursuit of certain kinds of research into the manipulation of the creation of living organisms. They would say that power could only legitimately be used in these situations to prevent the development and expansion of these powers. It is also readily conceivable that certain kinds of states could become so powerful, and at the same time so corrupt, that the only possible attitude to adopt toward them might be one of nonviolent noncooperation. The fact remains that an attitude of consistent passivity all along the line in the presence of a coercive power of which one does not approve is likely only to be ineffective, a way of contracting out of the situation. As we shall see, the passivity of Jesus in the presence of his opponents was of an entirely different character.

This attitude of consistent passivity is not normally advocated by those who argue for policies of nonviolent resistance to causes which are regarded as evil. Nonviolent action is the reverse of passive. To the extent that the nonviolent actors believe they can effectively influence those whom they oppose and, therefore, the situation in which both are involved, they are inevitably drawn into the area of political calculation; and politics is always about power and about the problems which power always brings. This may be a very civilized form of dealing with disputes and may have much to commend it on these grounds, but politics it remains. There are some circumstances in which the use of nonviolent methods can be a very effective powerploy. The situations in Gandhi's India and in Martin Luther King's black South provide examples of large groups of people who nonviolently resisted the wills of rulers, many of whom had a sensitive conscience and were answerable to a public which also had a sensitive conscience about the issues involved.

The question which anyone actively involved in human affairs has to face, therefore, is not how to avoid the contamination of power as much as possible, because power brings corruption and the likelihood of enslavement, but how to redeem power, facing its difficulties and using its opportunities so as to make peace—harmonious and constructive relationships.

A more negative argument also underlines the futility of attempting to avoid the problems that power brings by rejecting power itself. It has been said often enough that power corrupts. What is not said so often but is no less true is that the absence of power also corrupts, especially in situations where people have evaded its responsibilities or have become disappointed and frustrated because they have been denied it. In the nature of such cases, the corruption may become visible less quickly and may do less damage to others, but it will be no less malignant in its effect on those who suffer from the lack of power. All healthy people of sound mind and vigorously alive naturally desire to have a measure of power;[2] or if not power in itself, which so quickly becomes idolatrous, they desire the freedom, which is allied to power, to make decisions which shape events and have influence over other people whose cooperation in a common enterprise is sought. Nietzsche's conception of the will to power was damaged by his disproportionate emphasis upon it at the expense of other positive qualities, his distorted anti-Christianity and, perhaps, his excessive academic admiration for people of action. But he was right in celebrating the will to power's creative character. Something is lacking in individuals who, at crucial moments in their development, are not eager to embrace responsibility and the power which goes with it and to make the most of their talents, often appropriately called their "powers." If they are not willing to embrace responsibility, they are likely to be selfish, allowing others to carry its burdens when they should be doing so. If they refuse to make the most of their talents, they are merely lazy. Nietzsche was right also in seeing that those who lust after power and the rewards it brings, but who lose out in the struggle for it or who are not prepared to pay its price, readily become envious of those who succeed and self-righteous about its corrupting influence upon them. They become filled with resentment, breeding a slave mentality which, in its turn, makes them an easy prey to those who can exploit their weakness in the interest of their own will to power—Nietzsche's priests who batten upon life's failures. While there may be an element of perversity in his attack upon pity, on the ground that the pitiable are, as he alleges, only those who also long for power in their own unadmirable way (the power to hurt), even this insight further underlines the point that the lack of power brings problems no less than does its possession.

The relation between power and powerlessness, therefore, demands examination. Christian faith, as presented in the New Testament, provides a singularly illuminating exposure of the nature of that relationship and shows how many of its problems can be resolved. This is contrary to many popular notions and, of course, contradicts the claims of Nietzsche. The attitude of many Christians in Nietzsche's own time may have given a measure of plausibility to those claims, but he could hardly have misinterpreted the New Testament more radically than he did, and especially the teaching of the apostle Paul. In my judgment, nowhere does the subtlety, profundity, and strength of New Testament Christianity emerge more clearly than here, where it is often taken to be at its weakest.

Jesus himself confronts us in the Gospels, initially and in the final event, as a man of power, the lion of Judah who comes conquering and who will conquer. He appears as one who has authority, *exousia,* whose deeds, in contrast to those of the scribes and Pharisees, are as good as his words. At his touch, the demons tremble and are cast out and, as we shall see, in the fulfillment of his vocation he retains the initiative throughout. In this he stands firmly in the succession of the prophets, whose great exemplar is the mighty Elijah. It cannot be emphasized too strongly that his teaching about humility and about the necessity to exercise authority only in the form of a servant would have had no point and would have carried no conviction unless it had been delivered from a position of strength. We are told that after his rejection and death and when his exalted presence took leave of his followers, Jesus gave them a commission to preach the good news in all the creation with the assurance that all power would be given to them.

That power, *dynamis,* is vividly described as descending upon them on the day of Pentecost, a power so great that their human frames proved inadequate vessels to contain it, so that it burst forth from them in ecstatic utterance. That power also became the distinctive mark of the members of the first apostolic community, whose conception of its potential range became breathtakingly bold as their experience developed and as they had time to work out its implications. This is indicated by passages such as the first chapters of Ephesians and Colossians, and the second chapter of Philippians. In the Hellenistic world, people believed that life on this earth was dominated by "powers" that inhabited the upper air and claimed a determinative influence over human affairs. The apostolic community asserted that the power in the Spirit released by Jesus Christ was cosmic in its range and stronger than all of these "powers," that have to submit to his authority.

The New Testament possesses special significance for understanding the relation between power and powerlessness because, from the outset, the temptations of power and the possibilities of corruption within it were clearly recognized. Its emphasis on these temptations and possibilities may have been partly what misled Nietzsche. This is why Jesus exercised his ministry more and more as it developed through a voluntary abrogation of power. This was a matter of the most deliberate decision. Although we have plenty of evidence that he could have done otherwise had he so wished, Jesus allowed himself to be made captive and to be crucified as a rejected criminal, accepting the grim parody of being crowned as king only with thorns and of being lifted up above his fellows on a cross. Only those who have had it brought home to them in the most directly personal way that they have denied him and have no claim in themselves on the power of the Spirit are given apostolic authority.

Christians have always had to acknowledge that, since it is through crucifixion and death that Christ exercises his kingly office, all who claim to speak in his name must also exercise power in the form of a servant; but it goes so much against the natural grain that they have had the greatest difficulty in doing so. History abounds with examples both of the misuse and of the misunderstanding of power by Christians. The temptations which confront most Christians today are different from those which they faced in the heyday of Christendom, when social orders both in Eastern and Western Europe consciously strove to express the lordship of Christ. No doubt because their insight has been sharpened by the decline of their political influence in many countries in recent years, Catholic and Protestant churches have vied with one another in warning their members of the dangers of ecclesiastical triumphalism. Not much analysis, however, has been made concerning the subtlety and complexity of the relation between power and its abrogation, with the result that the guidance that is readily obtainable from reflection upon the New Testament has not been made accessible either to those who possess power or to those who lack it, both within the Christian community and in the wider life of society.

This weakness remains even in recent Christian writing about the relation between Christian faith and politics, where such analysis might reasonably be expected. The most substantial work of theology published in the last decade or so which deals with this relation is the trilogy of Jürgen Moltmann, *The Theology of Hope, The Crucified God,* and *The Church in the Power of the Spirit.*[3] Although he has much to say that is illuminating, at no point does he grapple with the complex implications of the possibility that some of those who are sustained by the hope of which he so eloquently speaks in his first volume may actually find their hopes realized. After all, the New Testament joyfully declares that what those who believe in Jesus Christ hope for is not only a promise for the future but also a reality already partially known in the Spirit. This means that those who are led by the Spirit have power, power which carries with it all the temptations inevitably attached to its possession, even for the most faithful servant of Christ. More than that, the greater the faithfulness, the greater the release of power and the more acute the problems. Like many other representatives of the currently fashionable "theology of liberation" and unlike Paul in writing to the Galatians, Moltmann does not consider how to avoid making newfound liberty an occasion for falling into a new kind of bondage. This is the more regrettable because he appears to think of liberation primarily in political terms, thus throwing into relief the issue of the relation between liberation and the power which quickly corrupts. The work of Reinhold Niebuhr would seem to be especially pertinent at this point. But even when Moltmann deals with the political implication of the acceptance of powerlessness by Jesus in the concluding chapter of *The Crucified God,* he appears unaware of all that Niebuhr wrote about the peculiar dangers facing those who exercise power with the conviction that their cause is the cause of righteousness.

Dietrich Bonhoeffer, in one of his letters from prison, speaks movingly of the redemptive nature of the powerlessness of Christ.[4] This was clearly important in the theological reinterpretation toward which Bonhoeffer was moving, but the reference is very brief and he was prevented from saying more. He mentions the way in which the Christian religion is always being "perverted into a form of privilege,"[5] but the use of the word "perverted" implies that this is a distortion that arises because of unfaithfulness. My contention will have to be that the matter is more complex and inescapable. Christian faith, as the Bible joyfully asserts, brings privileges that arise as a result of the work of grace; these cannot, therefore, be regarded as perversions. Bonhoeffer himself was a magnificent example of such a privileged person, having the internal resources to call upon and enjoy the riches of the Christian and European tradition in which he was steeped while he was imprisoned by the enemies of that tradition. Thus, even in physical bondage and under sentence of death, his spirit was supremely liberated. The issue of possible perversion arises when the question of these privileges' use is faced, in the light of the fact that they have been won only by Jesus' own voluntary abrogation of power. If Bonhoeffer had been allowed to escape execution and had become, as he surely would have, an influential leader of the German and ecumenical Christian community, he would then have had to consider how his own legitimate kind of Christian privilege was to avoid perversion. It is a question on which a closer examination of the vocation of Jesus should cast light.

6

The Vocation of Jesus
and Power

THE MINISTRY of Jesus is decisive for the Christian understanding of the relation between power and powerlessness. He worked out what that relation should be in terms of his own vocation within Israel and committed himself to it fully in his life and teaching, in his death, and in what issued from his death. His teaching was vindicated in action. No Christian should need instruction from Marxists that it is important not merely to understand but to change society; they have only to follow in the steps of Jesus.

Thus the question about the right use of power did not arise for Jesus in any speculative or academic way but strictly with reference to the question of how he could best fulfill his mission, a mission which arose out of his reflection upon the history of his people Israel —a nation with an exceptionally practical experience of the realities of power throughout its stormy history. Jesus himself cannot fail to have known from the outset that, on the ordinary human level, he possessed exceptional personal gifts. It is worth noting that before his ministry began he must have had experience in the voluntary restraint of power since he kept out of the public eye until he was thirty, almost middle age by the standards of the time. According to Luke's Gospel, his first utterance during his ministry, when he read from the sixty-first chapter of Isaiah in the synagogue (Luke 4:16–21), was a declaration that the liberating power of God promised by the prophets was now an active power in the midst of Israel. The story of his baptism also implies that he has been given unique powers from God for the fulfillment of his mission. He seems to speak as if by right with the kind of authority which a direct messenger of Israel's Lord might possess and not simply as an expositor or interpreter of a word which is to be distinguished from his own words. From the way in which the story is told, we have the impression that he may even have had some human difficulty in knowing how best to control the active power, *dynamis* rather than *exousia,* which flowed through him, particularly in his compassionate works of healing. In so far as it is possible to deduce from the Gospel what manner of human being as compared with other human beings Jesus was—and it should be remembered that the evangelists were not primarily interested in such questions— he appears as someone of vehement and sharply defined tempera- ment, expressing in his own person the inner spirit of the law and the prophets. Even if his denunciations of the rulers and leaders of the Jews reflect the attitudes of his followers as much as they do his own words, they could hardly have been recorded in that form unless at least some of their fire and passion derived from Jesus himself. What comes out particularly clearly from his ministry, as presented in different ways in all four of the Gospels, are his resolute and unshak- able independence—was anyone ever more inner-directed?—and his controlled mastery over events. It is he and not his opponents who holds the initiative throughout, and it is he who, when the time is ripe, forces the issue to its resolution.[1]

The teaching of Jesus presupposes that the presence of the kingdom means that quite enormous new strength, "the power of the age to come," is now present in the midst of humanity, so that those who share in that strength should conduct themselves with the confidence and assurance of the heirs of that kingdom. This is surely the main burden of the summary of that teaching given by Matthew in the Sermon on the Mount. The Sermon is misunderstood if it is taken to be a series of exhortations to use nonviolent methods as the best way of overcoming evil. It does commend nonviolence but, as we have already seen, it does so because the heirs of the kingdom are so strong that they do not need to resort to violence. The infinite resources of grace upon which they can call should enable them to conduct them- selves with gentleness of spirit, peaceableness, generosity, restraint, and freedom from anxiety. The promise held out to them is that they are able to accomplish the most difficult of achievements, to be the rich who can yet enter the kingdom of God.

Similarly, the Gospel of Luke, whose primary emphasis is upon a celebration of the kingly rule of Christ, is fitly prefaced by the Magnificat of Mary. This is often regarded as a hymn in praise of humility and a commendation of the justice of the downtrodden and oppressed's cause, including the joyful anticipation of their coming victory—a hymn which echoes the Song of Miriam in Exodus. Although it is all of these, it will be misinterpreted unless it is seen not only as an expression of the joy of a mother in Israel at having been chosen to be the mother of the Messiah but also as a celebration of the power of Israel's God, who is stronger than all the mighty of the earth. So strong is God that even the weak of the earth can be used to fulfill the divine purpose, scattering the proud in the imagination of their hearts, putting down the mighty from their seats, and exalting those of low degree.

The clearest indication that the ministry of Jesus did not bypass but directly faced the problems inherent in the handling of great power is provided by the remarkable story of his temptations, especially as told in the fourth chapter of Matthew, the chapter which is quickly followed by the Sermon on the Mount. The story is presented in stylized form, with the temptations coming in a careful succession and with Jesus answering the tempter's quotations from Scripture with profounder quotations from Deuteronomy. The latter may be intended as a reminder of Israel's test in the wilderness before being allowed to enter the Promised Land. This method of presentation should not conceal from us the intensity of the struggle which the story describes, a struggle which must have gone on for much longer than the traditional forty days before Jesus was ready to begin his public ministry. It is hard to see how the story could have been written, whatever editorial work may have been involved, except on the basis of Jesus' own personal account of that struggle.

The issue was about the power which Jesus knew he possessed and how it was to be used if his vocation to redeem Israel was to be fulfilled and not distorted. The attraction of the temptations lay in the fact that they were able plausibly to appeal to abilities which Jesus knew he had and which he would have been naturally eager to exercise. The first temptation, to turn the stones into bread, can be taken to symbolize the possibility of using his power to meet the obvious needs of people, as these needs presented themselves in ways which everyone could readily understand. In its concreteness, the Gospel tells us that this temptation came home to Jesus in the form of his own desperate hunger. It can hardly be doubted that Jesus was perfectly capable not only of providing himself with material sufficiency but also of doing the same for those within his human reach. The mysterious stories of the feeding of the multitudes imply as much, just as they also remind us that he was also ready to use his power to make bread available when the appropriate occasion arose. Where the temptation lay was in concentrating all of his power on this one end. To have done so would have obscured the real issue. Experience abundantly shows, even today, that when people's most urgent material needs are met, they immediately start clamoring for more and, unless they are called out of themselves by a more worthwhile purpose, turn angrily upon the providers when more is not readily forthcoming. They "murmur" in the way the children of Israel did in the wilderness and begin to sigh again for the fleshpots of Egypt, forgetting the captivity to alien taskmasters which went with them. If he had given in to this temptation, Jesus' redemptive mission would have been frustrated.

The second temptation can be thought of as that of the misuse of privilege. Although it is again presented in terms of Jesus' experience as an individual, it would have been understood by those to whom the story was addressed in terms of his position as representative of Israel, God's faithful servant people. Israel's temptation in this position, as the prophets had repeatedly warned, was that because of being singled out for the covenant relationship, Israel could automatically count on divine protection, no matter how ill-conceived the enterprise on which the nation was embarked might be. Jesus, the charismatic leader endowed with power from on high, as the immediately preceding story of his baptism had already emphasized, surely had the gifts, if anyone had, to lead his people to new heights of prosperity and influence. There is ample evidence, however, that there were many skeptics in Israel. Even though Jesus had been careful not to claim to be the Messiah, many must have cast doubt on the special destiny of Israel and even more on the claim of this carpenter's son from a provincial neighborhood to have any special part in the fulfillment of that destiny. What could have been more tempting than to demonstrate before such skeptics that he did indeed have the power which a special relationship to God carried with it and also to show this—on the basis of the promise of the psalmist—by a spectacular exhibition of his immunity from ordinary mortal hazards? Would not that serve to convince them of the reality of his own personal vocation and, much more important, of the vocation also of Israel as God's chosen people in the world?

Jesus sharply rejects this possibility as a "tempting" of God—a very strong idea. To tempt God was, in effect, to challenge God's right to be God, to demand that divinity be proved to our satisfaction according to criteria set up by ourselves. This means that we are trying to be rivals of God. Following this course, therefore, would be to make nonsense of Jesus' vocation. It would be to use his power as the servant of our own ambition rather than of God's will. In Paul's phrase, it would be to "count it a prize to be snatched at to be on an equality with God" (Phil. 2:6).

The final temptation is the most radical and, in consequence, the one which most directly raises the issue of the right use of power. Jesus possessed *exousia*. As one human being among others, and certainly by comparison with nearly all of his contemporaries in his small nation, he must have been conscious of having enormous power. He had magnetic gifts of leadership, he had healing charisma, and he was a supremely inspired teacher. What kind of man was this who produced his parables—with their amazing combination of unique originality of insight in a very special situation with directness of imagery—which have been able to speak to wise and simple alike across the ages and the continents? When the devil offered Jesus all of the kingdoms of the world and the glory of them, he was offering no more than what Jesus knew he had within himself to take over and possess. He had no need to shrink from such a prospect. Nor need the offer have been accepted in any crudely self-seeking way. Nothing would have been easier than to have put himself forward as a representative of the best of Israel's religious heritage in such a way as to win the cooperation of the dominant groups in Israel, the scribes and the Pharisees. After all, on many matters their teaching was rather similar, and they had a common concern for the religious well-being of the people. It is hinted at more than once in the Gospels, but notably in the encounter with Nicodemus, that attempts may have been made to find and build on common ground and, with a little give-and-take on both sides, should it not have been possible? Likewise, someone with Jesus' skill in relationships and in argument could surely have contrived to win at least the tolerance of the Roman authorities. If a contentious fellow like Paul was able to proclaim him later as Lord and king over humankind to the gentile world after he had been shamefully crucified as a criminal, should not he himself, at the height of his powers, have been able to win a larger national and international following? And should he not have been able to do this without having to create that rift between Jews and his own followers which has done so much damage right up to our own day? Even more than that, could he not have used his gifts to set forth an ideal of humanity which harmonized the best of the Jewish and the Greek traditions, as so many of his followers have tried to do since his day, without all the dubious accompaniments of apparent claims to divinity, sacrifice, atonement, and resurrection which always have been stumbling blocks to the Jews and foolishness to the Greeks? When Jesus was shown the kingdoms of this world and the glory of them, he must have known that he had the potential to become the leader of that true humanism, that religion of humanity, which has always seemed the most attractive of prospects to self-consciously enlightened people, to people of goodwill. Modern Christian liberalism has often tried to see and present Jesus in this way and has been embarrassed when it has been argued that the New Testament, and classical orthodoxy in most Christian traditions, sees him differently. Why did Jesus not set himself up as a kind of combination of, for example, Socrates, Francis of Assisi, Shakespeare, Abraham Lincoln, Florence Nightingale, Gandhi, and Martin Luther King? And why did he not do this in such a way as to make it easy to harmonize his teaching with the forms of other religions that are acceptable to modern Western people—with liberal Judaism, Buddhism, and Taoism? Would this not have been the true ecumenism that the universities and the foundations could support without reservation? Is not the "scandal of particularity" a real scandal to all right-minded people? Yet Jesus rejected this temptation as the most insidious and deadly, to be repelled by the invocation of the first and greatest commandment itself. Why?

The reason for this rejection is that it would have contradicted the unique insight into humanity's relation to God which Jesus came to reveal. It is an insight we cannot possess until, like the people of Jesus' own time, we also are scandalized by it. He saw that the devil's offering could be accepted only by the denial of God. The power that Jesus possessed did not originate from within himself as an exceptionally gifted human being. It was a belief current in the mythology of his time that this world was under the sway of alien powers. This meant that the only terms upon which the kingdoms of this world and their glory could be offered to Jesus were by his submission to the devil or Satan,[2] as the story explicitly says. The implication was that Jesus would have to agree that they were gifts from Satan. But the distinctiveness of Jesus' vocation lay in his clear recognition of the meaning of the first commandment: that the Lord alone is God and that it is to God alone that the scepter and the crown belong. He had to make his people see how they had denied the Lord this glory, as a necessary condition of their liberation from Satan's grip. This led him to see that it was impossible to give the people direct leadership or to build upon whatever measure of earthly authority they might be persuaded to grant him. He had to take the form of a servant, as Second Isaiah had foretold. The creation cannot take the place of the Creator. For Jesus to have tried, as Satan tempted him, would have been to confess that he himself had misunderstood his own mission. He would, in fact, have become no more than yet another "captain appointed to lead his people back to the captivity of Egypt." When he isolated and decisively rejected this final temptation, Jesus had reached human maturity and was ready to begin his public ministry.

That the final temptation is rightly understood in this sense receives confirmation from the fact that an acute awareness of the importance of a responsible use of power, together with a no less acute awareness of the difficulty of achieving it, is present in the accounts we have of the training of the Twelve. The sons of Zebedee were probably the most explicit of Jesus' disciples in acknowledging how hard they found it to accept authority in the form of a servant. They must have been enormously impressed with the power flowing from Jesus and the exciting possibilities it held, possibilities in which they might reasonably have hoped to share and from which they could have expected to derive benefit. The prospect of sitting on thrones judging Israel would have been all the more dazzling by contrast with the actual conditions they were meeting daily as his followers—having left home, kindred, and work in order to be with him. The fact that the disciples discovered that they themselves also possessed some of

Jesus' healing charisma would have inflated their spirits still further, so that they had to be warned to rejoice not that the spirits were subject to them but that their names were written in heaven. The difficulty they must have experienced in the presence of the radicalism of Jesus' claim is shown, perhaps most vividly, in the fourth Gospel's account of how, when its full impact came home to his followers, many of them walked with him no more, so that he challenged the Twelve themselves with the invitation to do the same.[3]

For the right understanding of the relation between power and powerlessness in the ministry of Jesus, it is essential to see that acceptance of the passion leading to his death was itself the most conscious and resolute exercise of power. Jesus did not go up to meet his death as the passive victim of powers greater than he himself was able to cope with. On the contrary, he set his face to go up to Jerusalem, knowing that in doing so he was deliberately forcing the issue. The probability is that, until he did so, he had decided that the time was not ripe, which would account for the way in which he had kept clear of the authorities in obscure neighborhoods where he would not have attracted very much attention. It was only after he had sized up the situation that he came to the conclusion that there was no alternative to direct confrontation. Although it was as dangerous for them as it was for him, the representatives of Israel had now to make up their minds where they stood in relation to him and to his vocation.

Far from being a form of passive resistance, Jesus' method is one of active initiative to precipitate decision, thrusting responsibility back onto the shoulders of those who would have gone to great lengths to avoid it. Both Luke and John in their different fashions tell the story of his passion itself, where he might appear to have reached the point of allowing events to take their course, in such a way as to bring this out. He does not abjure but reserves his power. He refuses to exercise it in any way which will deflect him from his vocation and thus enable those involved to escape their own responsibility in relation to that vocation—a vocation in which they share because it is that of Israel as God's servant. This is the point of his rebuke to the disciple who cut off the ear of the high priest's servant at the time of his arrest. As Jesus said, if he wished, could he not have called on far greater resources, far more powerful armaments, than the swords of his followers (Matt. 26:51–53)?

The powerlessness of Jesus was deliberately chosen to make clear once and for all the depth of the estrangement of his people and, through them, of humankind from God, the source of their life. In so doing, Jesus was able also to expose the dishonesty of our claim to exercise power in a way that makes us possessors of our own souls, autonomous beings who are not answerable to anyone else for the way we act and who do not need to depend on God's grace. As we have seen, Jesus had a strong "will to power" and was able to call on great resources of power; but his temptation had taught him that the "will to power" had to be transcended before sinful human beings could be entrusted with it. He demonstrated this by voluntarily refusing to exercise the power which he possessed and by allowing those who believed that they were able to use properly the powers granted to them without having to transcend themselves, to do what they would with him, the Lord's faithful servant. This revealed decisively the corrupt and destructive nature of power centered only on humanity, including that derived from the faith of Israel itself.

It is wrong, therefore, to conclude that Jesus provides any justification for the weak and ineffectual to suppose that, because of their weakness and ineffectiveness, they are more righteous than the strong and the competent. If he had provided such a justification, those who like Nietzsche charge him and his followers with fomenting the resentment of the weak would have reasonable ground for complaint. That resentment is as damaging in its own way as the proud misuse of power. It is, in fact, the obverse of the same attitude. What Jesus does provide is a radical critique of the will to power, which clears the way for its proper use.

Jesus worked out this critique of the will to power not in theoretical terms, but in the clash of wills which led to his passion and death. The passion narrative seems to seize every opportunity to make this clear. It is worth noting that Jesus accepted and did not repudiate the kingly role which was ascribed to him, but that he did so in a disarmingly ironical and almost humorous way. This is the kind of attitude that would only have been possible for someone who knew that he had great reserves of power on which to draw.

It is not entirely inappropriate to see the passion story in one of its aspects as a way of deflating the pretentiousness which seems inseparable from the human use of power, especially when it is allied to religious claims. Thus, Jesus does enter Jerusalem as a king, not on a noble charger, but on a donkey's back; and the crowd whose plaudits he acknowledges is a small group of insignificant followers and of excited children in the Temple. Before entering, Jesus presides at a meal of the inner circle of his disciples, which might legitimately make them anticipate the great Messianic banquet where they might be tempted to envisage themselves as the rulers of the twelve tribes of a reconstituted Israel. However, Jesus tells them that the bread and wine represent his broken body and his blood poured out,[4] and he warns them that one of their own number will take the initiative in handing him over to alien powers.[5] When Jesus is brought formally before the rulers of the people, we are told that he held his peace instead of confronting his accusers and using the opportunity to justify his teachings and his mission by a brilliant display of advocacy that would have been well within his power. Jesus' silence accuses his judges more effectively than any words, because they are unable to maintain silence and thus stand condemned out of their own mouths. He is ultimately crowned as king of the Jews, but in mockery. His throne is a cross and his crown one of thorns. It is hard to envisage a more savage rejection by the possessors of earthly power or a more complete exposure of the hollowness of their claims to rule.

The story of the agony in Gethsemane, which is told as a preface to the final events of Jesus' life, also implies that his acceptance of passion and death was not due to his weakness but to his strength. The bitterness of his anguish arose from his awareness of wasted potentiality, not so much in himself as an individual, but in his people as representative of humanity. Why are we so foolish and obstinate that we refuse to be saved except in the hardest possible way? Humankind at its best—in the people of the covenant and their appointed leaders—can have no use for the one called to interpret and fulfill their vocation in all its richness, except to reject and to destroy him. His attitude is contrasted with that of his disciples who, in their human weakness, are unable to watch with him one hour and fall into unconsciousness and therefore into irrelevance.

It is in the setting of his strength that his enigmatic cry from the cross recorded in Matthew and Mark, "My God, my God, why hast thou forsaken me," has to be understood. This is the lowest point reached by Jesus in his voluntary abrogation of power, but it loses significance unless it is seen in the context of the whole of his mission. Like the psalmist in the opening words of Psalm 22, which this cry echoes, Jesus on the point of death is still speaking as representative of Israel, the Lord's chosen servant. We know that Israel's idea of the divine favor was realistic and explicit. It meant riches, honor, and length of days, seeing the goodness of the Lord in the land of the living. There is no evidence that Jesus regarded this as mistaken, although his teaching about the perils of riches makes it abundantly clear that he knew how easily it could be oversimplified. He would not have entertained the notion that the divine favor might mean only suffering, deprivation, and passivity in the presence of those of evil will. If he had thought that, his cry from the cross would have been completely unintelligible. He accepted his betrayal and agony as part of his trial, the test which he told his followers in the Lord's Prayer to pray that they might be spared, as he himself appears to have prayed in Gethsemane. The significance of the cry of dereliction lies in its recognition that God has now decisively withdrawn the divine favor from Israel. Why?

It is a question to which there is no human answer. This is made all the more clear because Jesus alone of all humankind had the right to ask it. If any other member of the empirical Israel had asked it, many obvious answers might have been given for God's rejection, as the prophets had frequently warned people at many points in their history. Even the cry of the psalmist in Psalm 22 cannot be taken with the seriousness which attaches to the cry from the cross. The psalmist's cry is, after all, part of a poem, "emotion recollected in tranquillity," which goes on to celebrate the fact that God did not prove to have forsaken that particular servant. Jesus is at the point of death. According to all human experience and in contrast even to his closest Old Testament precursor, Job, there was no longer any prospect of his ever being able to see the goodness of the Lord in the land of the living. His life has come to an end with a tremendous question mark set against all human endeavor. This includes his own endeavor, undertaken in utter faithfulness to a God-given vocation and with every effort made, with unparalleled restraint, to avoid the misuse of the power which was made available for the fulfillment of that vocation. In obedience to the Father, Jesus had identified himself with his people—the people whom God had called out from among the nations to be his people. These people decisively rejected Jesus and spurned the power which he brought with him. When confronted by their true king, they cried, "We have no king but Caesar," the symbol of this-worldly power. Why?

Since no answer to this question is possible in ordinary human terms, it can only be dealt with if an effort is made to do justice to its radicalism. The superficial explanation that Jesus became disillusioned when he realized there was going to be no last-minute reprieve from death, hardly merits mention. Jesus had chosen this way deliberately and had prophesied that it would lead to his death, and this cry is after all part of the gospel, the good news that his death was not the end. What has to be seen is that the cry of dereliction is not a cry of unbelief. Jesus is not questioning God's reality; he is asking why God has chosen to forsake the faithful servant.

It is of the utmost significance for our understanding of the relation between power and powerlessness, as it is indeed for our understanding of the whole human condition, that no answer is given to Jesus' question from within life as we all normally know it or of the possibilities which life has within it. The answer comes only from Jesus himself when he goes into the darkness of death and when he appears after his death to those who had shared some of his earthly ordeals and who became the recipients of his Spirit. The question and the answer became, in the end, an exchange only between Jesus and the Father, in which all the rest of humankind had no part. "No man knows the Son save the Father," says Matthew. Karl Barth has called this "the darkest and deepest word in Scripture."[6] The dereliction represents the surrender of God to the state of man, a self-surrender in which "he does not cease to be God but yet makes the state and fate of man his own in such a way that his divine existence for all other eyes than his own becomes absolutely invisible."[7]

This tremendous fact has implications along the whole range of human understanding in relation to God. It throws light, for example, on what we choose to call our unbelief. The dereliction and the cross declare that there is only one human being who has ever truly believed in God and that, in the ultimate crisis, his faith was invisible to all human eyes. The dereliction and cross declare not so much that "God is dead" as that the belief that humankind claims to cherish in God is a self-deception. In relation to our particular theme, it means that all human structures of power, including those of Israel, the people of the covenant, are thrown into disarray. Even the strongest of us are put out of countenance. "There is none righteous, no, not one." This is true not only of individuals but also of all human institutions. Whatever is to be made at this time of the story of the rending of the veil of the Temple, its symbolism is clear enough. It symbolizes the most radical judgment on all forms of human activity, including what might be held to be the most invulnerably holy. There is no place on earth, not even the holy of holies where the ark of the covenant dwells—the very fount of spiritual power in the eyes of Israel—which can make any human action authentic or give it sanction. Jesus has been rejected by those who maintain the power structures of this world, ecclesiastical and civil, and rejected in such a way as to conceal the real nature of the threat which he posed to their autonomy—that of the Lord himself in judgment. Nor were those who were not part of those power structures in any better situation. The crowd also turned against him, while his disciples and his family also disassociated themselves from him at the end.

A proper understanding of the present relation between power and powerlessness is not possible unless the full extent of the judgment passed on all human power by Jesus' acceptance of powerlessness is seen. Every form of human power becomes precarious, spiritual as well as political and military, revolutionary as well as reactionary, liberationist as well as repressive, liberal as well as conservative, the subtle power of the apparently weak as well as the blatant power of the obviously strong. All are bound up together in the sinfulness of humanity in the presence of the rejected and crucified Christ. No one and no group can claim exemption. Even "the quiet in the land," those who wait for the consolation of Israel, have to see that they are at best merely irrelevant. Jesus was alone with the Father, and any righteousness which may come to them derives from that relationship and not from anything in themselves.

Therefore, anyone who claims the authority of Jesus for any one side in any human struggle for power without the most careful and self-critical qualification has not come to terms with the meaning of his dereliction and death. As we shall go on to emphasize, this includes those whose cause is, on an ordinary human level, one which would be widely agreed to be righteous, as well as those in whose cause the element of self-interest at the expense of others is more obviously present. It even includes those causes which, as some modern theologians claim for revolutionary or reformist movements, are conscious efforts to express the liberating power of Christ himself, and which Christian people undertake in the sincere conviction that they are interpreting the guidance of the Spirit in doing so. This conviction may strengthen their resolution but, at the same time, it should warn them that the causes remain their own causes. Their successful pursuit means the acceptance of a measure of power on their own part, and all power is corruptible, including that exercised by the most well-intentioned Christian in the best of causes. Even the best of causes is never purely righteous. Jesus, whose cause was the most purely righteous, seemed to all human eyes to be forsaken by God. All of us, therefore, have to scrutinize our pursuit of righteousness in the light of his human powerlessness.

This matters directly in dealing with what we call practical affairs. It is the reverse of a marginal pious comment to be heeded, if at all, only when the pressure of a struggle for power is relaxed or as a reminder to show a measure of magnanimity to a defeated enemy after such a struggle. It is emphatically not a piece of what self-important politicians describe patronizingly as "theology," by which they mean principles of such generality that they need not be taken into account in making day-to-day decisions. On the contrary, no one and no group can be trusted with power, no matter now righteous their cause, who have not had it brought home to them at the core of their beings that the rejection and crucifixion of Christ expresses God's judgment on all exercises of power. Just as it was only after Abraham had been compelled to raise the knife to slay Isaac that he became fit to be entrusted with the responsibility of being the father of his people, so it is only after we have been shamed and humbled by the powerlessness of the powerful Jesus, reigning as king from the cross, that any of us can dare to exercise any significant power over others.

This means more than that we must be prepared to answer to God for the way in which our power is used. The powerful are often not reluctant to acknowledge that. It can be made to add dignity and weight to their exercise of power and sometimes to provide an impressive excuse for their not being answerable to their neighbors on levels where such accountability is appropriate. It means that God has destroyed all pretentiousness attached to the human use of power. It can be exercised only in fear and trembling, but also with a measure of ironic detachment about our presumption in taking it upon ourselves to impose our wills upon our fellows or upon the processes of nature. It carries the recognition that we need not only to be self-critical, but also to be open to the criticism of our neighbors, since we know that we cannot trust ourselves to be disinterested critics. And this is true not only of individuals in relation to their own exercise of power but also of the way in which they discharge their responsibilities as representatives of communities.

Mature Christians and the Power of the Spirit

> "True, he died on the cross in weakness, but he lives by the power of God; and we who share his weakness shall by the power of God live with him in your service."
>
> 2 Cor. 13:4, NEB

THE ABROGATION of earthly power by Jesus and the divine judgment on all earthly exercises of power was carried through right to the bitter end. Jesus died, and the realistic Jewish people knew as well as anyone else that you cannot be deader than dead. The memory and example of a death can be an influence in human affairs, but a dead person can have no power of initiative. The broken, lifeless body of Jesus was laid in the tomb, and the tomb was sealed.

According to the Book of Acts, the overturning of this, which gave birth to the distinctive Christian faith, came home to the followers of Jesus most vividly on the day of Pentecost. God's Spirit came upon them as a great onrush of new power, power which was so over- whelming that their human frames were unable to contain and channel it. Why the resurrection experiences themselves do not have a link with power to the same extent is not explained. We are told in the fourth Gospel that the risen Christ breathed upon his disciples and imparted the Holy Spirit to them, promising that this carried with it the power to loose and to bind (John 20:22–23). But this could well be a reading back from post-pentecostal experience when the new power had had time to be partially assimilated and expressed and when the apostolic community had had an opportunity to learn its effectiveness in overcoming other spirits which resisted it.

The most striking aspect of the accounts of the resurrection appearances in the synoptic Gospels with reference to power is their reserve. The appearances are made for the most part only to those who had been followers of Jesus during his earthly ministry, but they are curiously fitful and almost inconsequential. Sufficient assurance is given that it is really he and none other who appears, but his followers are sharply warned to keep their distance from him until his ascension. This is also true of the fourth Gospel. The resurrection appearances are signs, telling Jesus' followers that the crucifixion was not the end, that Jesus as the Christ still lives, and that God's action in him continues. The appearances have a preparatory character, making the apostolic community ready for the coming of the Spirit. The purpose of the warnings not to come too close to the risen Christ might then be to keep them away from the power which emanates from him, for fear that they be consumed by it. Thus, when Thomas in the fourth Gospel refuses to accept this but demands to see the wounds in Jesus' hands and side, wounds which in the symbolism of that Gospel represent the cost of our redemption, the experience overwhelms him. Some scholars have argued that this story, with its concluding statement that those who have not had to see but who believe are fortunate, is the climax of the Gospel. According to the way in which Luke tells the story, the ascension was necessary because the power which had been concentrated in the human Jesus returned to its source in order to be diffused through humankind and made available more widely to his followers in a measure adjusted to normal human capacity. Even so, the impact of the descent of the Spirit on the day of Pentecost was massive.

The pentecostal story is so familiar and is usually considered so much a part of distinctively "religious" experience that it may require an adjustment of the imagination to think of it as an account of the access of power which carried with it the same consequences as every other access of power. When this is realized, the contrast between the pentecostal experience and what happened on the cross becomes all the more striking. As Jüngel has reminded us in his book on death,[1] death means relationlessness, the loss of direction, the end of the story, emptiness. Yet through the death of Jesus, power is released to create a new set of relationships stronger than any previously known, a burst of illumination which makes possible a fresh interpretation of what has gone before, the beginning of a new story and overflowing fulfillment. It was from this access of power that the Christian church arose as an historical community, a power which became available only through the acceptance of powerlessness by Jesus. The church today is not likely to understand its nature nor its mission unless full and equal weight is given to both of these facts.

It is particularly important to remember this when the big distinction between the vocation of Jesus and that of the Spirit-filled community is considered. His vocation, although directed from the outset toward that of the people of Israel with whom he identified himself, was unique and that of an individual. He gathered disciples around him, but as his ministry moved toward its climax, his loneliness became more marked until, on the cross, he was stripped of all earthly relationships. The Spirit, on the other hand, was given in the first instance to a community, "when they were all together in one place," and it was only in relationship with one another that they realized the Spirit's power. The more they learned of the Spirit, the more obvious it became that it was inadequate to think of themselves as an association of separate individuals who contracted together to work as Christ's body in the world. The unity they possessed, they derived from him in the Spirit. They found it as they participated in the life of his body. They did not bring it with them as a contribution to the life of the body. "The new man in Christ" of which they spoke was not an idealized individual, but the new humanity discovered only in relationship. Any special power given to an individual, what the apostles called a "gift" of the Spirit, was entrusted to him or her for the sake of the community and could find fulfillment only in the life of the community, needing always to be supplemented by gifts granted to others. From the outset, as the stories in the early chapters of the Book of Acts tell, anyone who was tempted to use gifts only for their own advantage or at the expense of others invited retribution. The extent of the mutual dependence of all the members of the body of Christ is given classic statement in 1 Corinthians 12, which is followed in the succeeding chapter by the celebration of the primacy of agape or divine love. It is also stated in a wider context in Ephesians 4, where it is related specifically to the self emptying into powerlessness and the consequent fulfillment of the crucified, risen, and exalted Christ.

These three points need to be noted at this stage of our argument about the nature of the power of the Spirit. First, that power is as far-reaching as it is intense. Christian revivalism has emphasized the latter and Christian institutionalism the former, but both need to have justice done to them and traditional ways of thinking about both probably need revision. With the freedom from false idealization which marked the account of the founding of the church in the Book of Acts from the very outset, we are told that those on whom the Spirit descended had to face the charge immediately that this was no more than another outburst of religious hysteria, only too similar to intoxication. That was not surprising. What was surprising was the ease and the common sense (Acts 2:15) with which they were able to rebut the charge and the speed with which they learned to distinguish between what was of enduring quality and what was transitory in the experience which had overtaken them. They did not spend all of their time celebrating what had befallen them or trying to recapture the original excitement. They knew that it meant that they had fresh work to do, and they began at once with their tasks of healing, teaching, and proclamation. In particular, they discovered that the Spirit's presence made possible a greatly enriched set of relationships with each other, which yet allowed their community to be open to any who were able to join.[2] What is perhaps even more remarkable is the way in which the infant church, still tiny and insignificant by any external standard, found the power which gave it the confidence and independence of spirit to break out of the tightly enclosed community of the old Israel and, in the very first generation of its life, to share its faith and all the variety and depth of relationships which it brought with other people of many nations in many places scattered throughout the gentile world. Even more, the first Christians were impelled by their new faith to set the church in such a universal context that they were able to produce a new system of thought in which the crucified and rejected Christ became the head of a new creation, "far above all principality, and power, and might, and dominion, and every name that is named . . ." (Eph. 1:21, AV).

The sheer audacity of this last claim has not always been sufficiently appreciated by modern Christians, nervously anxious lest their recognition of it might imply their commitment to the picture of the physical universe which is presupposed in passages like the first chapters of Colossians and Ephesians. We must, of course, try to demythologize, but we are unlikely to hear a living word for our time unless we have first made an imaginative effort to recapture the liberating power of the original insight which prompted the first Christians to create the myth. It was surely a unique experience of power which led the author of Ephesians to write:

> I pray that the God of our Lord Jesus Christ, the all-glorious Father, may give you the spiritual powers of wisdom and vision, by which there comes the knowledge of him. I pray that your inward eyes may be illumined, so that you may know what is the hope to which he calls you, what the wealth and glory of the share he offers you among his people in their heritage, and how vast the resources of his power open to us who trust in him. They are measured by his strength and might which he exerted in Christ when he raised him from the dead, when he enthroned him at his right hand in the heavenly realms, far above all government and authority, all power and dominion, and any title of sovereignty that can be named, not only in this age but in the age to come. He put everything in subjection beneath his feet, and appointed him as supreme head to the church, which is his body and as such holds within it the fullness of him who receives the entire fullness of God (Eph. 1:17–23, NEB).

Our very different picture of the physical universe and of its relation to human affairs may make it difficult for us to know how to interpret such a passage today, but this at least is as clear as it ever was. It could not have been written except by someone who had known an enormous access of power, power which had enabled him or her to see hitherto undreamed of possibilities for human beings. We have already noted that it was widely believed in the Hellenistic world of New Testament times that the universe was inhabited by "powers" which were stronger than ordinary human beings on their own and which influenced human lives directly and on unconscious and subconscious levels. These "powers" had an identity so definite as to be self-authenticating. They were so strong that they could only be challenged indirectly. It has been suggested that the nearest modern analogies to them might be the complex of sentiments, desires, and loyalties together with the ideologies which try to explain and justify them, which gather round such notions as those of race, nationality, class, or sex. It is hard to be confident that this is a true analogy, but it does seem to be clear that the "powers" presented themselves to the people of New Testament times as entities with an independent reality. People were convinced also that, on their own unaided resources, they lacked the strength to shake off the dominance of these "powers." This makes all the more impressive the apostolic conviction that the risen Christ was stronger than all the powers and that his Spirit had released gifts that enabled them to share in that strength. This was liberation indeed! As Paul declared ecstatically at the climax of his great argument in Romans 8, those who possess the Spirit have all the privileges of God's children; they are heirs who are able to be God's agents in emancipating the natural creation from its bondage (Rom. 8:18–23).

Christians throughout the ages have performed this office with varying degrees of faithfulness and success. To the extent that they have genuinely shared the apostolic conviction, however, it can be said that they have found that the Spirit has continued to be powerful along the whole range of life. Performing this office has brought them into inevitable contact with the dominant powers of this world. The result of that contact has varied and the attitude of the Christian community toward the alien powers has varied. Within the confines of the New Testament itself, Paul's attitude toward the Roman authorities was one of respect, while that of the Book of Revelation was one of hostility. But there has always been contact, and the more vigorously people have committed themselves to the Spirit of Christ, the more active its power has been and the more the powers of this world have been compelled to respond, whether by redoubled opposition or by submission.

It can be further claimed that any authentic rediscovery of the power of the Spirit is likely to bring with it a fresh understanding of the extent of the sphere in which the lordship of Christ is meant to be expressed. The rise of the ecumenical movement among the churches in this century provides an illustration of this. It is worth recalling this at a time when the movement is in danger of being reduced either to becoming merely the expression of one political "power" among others or to being a series of attempts to merge denominational organizations with one another. The movement arose in the first instance because people deeply committed to the worldwide missionary enterprise saw that any genuine unity of the people of God must be deep as well as broad, and that it must affect their internal relations as well as their efforts to evangelize others. They also saw that it must be a force working for the liberation of all parts of life from bondage to alien powers, and not merely those which came under ecclesiastical jurisdiction. The great series of statements and papers produced in connection with the Oxford and Edinburgh Conferences in 1937, the Amsterdam Assembly of 1948, and the Evanston Assembly of 1954, many of which inspired some of the most creative social and political actions of the postwar period, make this very clear. The drive of the power of the Spirit is toward a greater and more inclusive community.

What remains essential today as in apostolic times is that the liberation which the Spirit brings, and the community which it calls into being, should continue to be understood in distinctively Christian terms. In the first instance this means that Christians should be acutely aware of the dangers which emerge precisely at the point where success is achieved. Faith should indeed inspire movements toward political or cultural liberation from the domain of alien powers, whether those powers are expressed in human or in less palpable form. It may also sometimes lead Christians to support or participate in such movements even though their initial inspiration may not spring from within the Christian community itself. But faith will never allow itself to be driven into the absolutist position which the majority of such movements, especially when their primary goals are political, are always tempted to claim for themselves. When this happens, no matter how good the cause may be, the alien powers rather than the Spirit of Christ have triumphed.

Christians who understand the source of their own power will know that all successful liberation movements quickly create new forms of privilege and engender a spirit of exclusiveness. They will also know that the better the cause for which they have fought, the easier it becomes to find a self-righteous justification for those forms and that spirit. The opponents of the triumphant movement, or those who stood aside from the struggle, are denied their rights or they are ostracized, even in relation to matters which were not in contention. The Christian community has had to learn slowly and painfully through the ecumenical movement that the only way to heal the old wounds which long-divided churches have inflicted on one another is for each to listen patiently to the other and for them to consider one another, "seeking the agreements in their differences and the differences in their agreements." They should see that the same principle applies in dealing with matters which, in these days, become contentious more quickly than those of relations between long-divided churches: those between people of different race and national groups, and even between men and women. The challenge of the inclusiveness of the Spirit of Christ is no less direct in those fields than it is in that of interchurch relations.

That many people who hold strong convictions will not find it easy to meet that challenge underlines the importance of the second observation which has to be made about the power of the Spirit. However intense and far-reaching, however triumphant in its consequences the power which the Spirit brings may be, it always remains that of the rejected, crucified, powerless Jesus. Furthermore, it is of the nature of this fact that the Spirit-sustained community itself can never take it for granted. It is a perpetual challenge and offense, and the more successful the church is in obedience to the Spirit, the more acutely it will continue to feel the sting of the challenge. When that sting diminishes, that is a sure sign that the reality of Christ in the Spirit is being distorted or ignored. No matter how much prosperity a church enjoys and no matter how much power it wields, it cannot survive as a community of the Spirit unless it constantly returns to the foot of the cross. And it is not likely genuinely to return unless it finds it extremely hard to do it. Christ's body is a broken body, even when it is serving him effectively. His blood is our life, but it is blood which was poured out for our sakes. In John Owen's phrase, the fruit of the Spirit is that of a tree whose root is in the grave of Christ.

While this is a truth which it is never easy to see, it may be a little less difficult for churches to acknowledge it in days like these than it has been at some other periods in history, because the churches often meet widespread indifference and hostility even in communities where they have previously known success. What some Christians appear to find hard to see is that a similar temptation to avoid the challenge of this fact also arises when they commit themselves to the service of causes in the general life of society which may have more obviously attractive claims to "righteousness" than those of unpopular ecclesiastical institutions.

We noted earlier that the Beatitude in the Sermon on the Mount which promises possession of the earth to those "of gentle spirit" or "the meek" immediately precedes that Beatitude which says that those who hunger and thirst that the right shall prevail will be satisfied. The passion that the right should prevail is vital. Its possession is one of the most precious fruits of the Spirit. Jesus also promises that this passion will be satisfied. To the extent that it will be satisfied, however, it will be open to the corrupting influence of success, and it will probably produce fresh unrighteousness. This is why it is essential that those who have this passion should also have a gentle spirit. Although the apostle may not have had the connection definitely in mind when he juxtaposed the two Beatitudes, experience confirms that a passion for righteousness that is not linked with a gentle spirit is peculiarly dangerous. In the past it has led to ecclesiastical tyranny, and it still does on the margins of the modern world or in religious but non-Christian societies where conviction of a divine sanction hardens the heart against offenders. More commonly, it leads to political tyranny, especially by those who have won power precariously after a hard struggle. It becomes irresistible for them to use the ostensible righteousness of their cause and the very passion with which they fought for it as a reason for behaving unjustly toward others and, of course, especially toward their defeated opponents.

Although the Jews had a more highly developed passion for righteousness than that of any other nation, and although they were not slow to identify God's cause with their own, it was a sign that grace was present in the Old Testament as well as in the New when the psalmist was able to look forward to the day of the Lord as a time in which "mercy and truth are met together, righteousness and peace have kissed each other" (Ps. 85:10, AV). Until that day comes in its fullness, however, this harmonious relation will only be achieved approximately and always with struggle against opposition, both from within those seeking mercy, truth, righteousness, and peace and from others who have more interest in emphasizing one of those qualities rather than the others. Only the knowledge that whatever degree of righteousness we possess we owe to the Lord, who was unable to count on any human cooperation in winning his victory for righteousness, will enable any of us to achieve even that approximation.

The place in the New Testament where this is most clear in the developing experience of the church is, perhaps, in the remarkable exchanges between Paul and the Corinthians—the most gifted, powerful, and therefore the most vulnerable of all the early Christian communities. Paul is obviously attached to this church because its members are so gifted, but he is driven to deep frustration by the way in which they allow their very gifts to obscure the source of their power and thus to lead them astray. This is why, at the outset of his first letter, he tells them that "this doctrine of the cross is sheer folly to those on their way to ruin, but to us who are on the way to salvation it is the power of God" (1 Cor. 1:18 NEB). This is why he reminds them that "divine folly is wiser than the wisdom of men, and divine weakness stronger than man's strength." He goes on to say: "To shame the wise, God has chosen what the world counts folly, and to shame what is strong, God has chosen what the world counts weakness. . . . The word I spoke, the gospel I proclaimed . . . carried conviction by spiritual power, so that your faith might be built not upon human wisdom but upon the power of God" (1 Cor. 1:27—2:5 NEB). Unless they see this, their very gifts will themselves become divisive. Instead of fulfilling their proper function of nourishing the whole body, so that it grows in strength, they weaken and damage it. The reason for this has already been made clear. Gifts bring power, and the exercise of power always carries an element of self-assertion. As Paul says to the Corinthians in his second letter, they are quick to imply that this is true on his part in his relation with them (2 Cor. 10), but they do not see how it also applies to themselves. Unless this self-assertion is checked and disciplined by agape, that is, divine love, it creates a clash of power, which produces competition, rivalry, and in the end strife and the breakdown of the unity of the body—the denial of all that the gospel has made possible. Paul had to tell them that this was already beginning to happen with sects and parties being formed, at best like political partisans and at worst like idolaters (1 Cor. 3:3–7).

Paul's experience with the Corinthians also helps to underline the importance of the kind of observation which has to be made about power within the Christian community. Its communal nature magnifies the difficulties of handling it aright. This is our third point. Nietzsche's "will to power" gains much of its impressiveness from the fact that he presents it in terms of the strong individual who is able to dominate others. Groups are there to be led or controlled by such an individual or, in their weak-willed resentment, they huddle together to try to find protection in each other for their mediocrity. They cannot defeat the individual with a strong will to power. Only another, with a stronger will, can do that. The fact that life does often work out like that is a reminder that nothing is more ambitious, indeed foolhardy, than the Christian attempt to harmonize spiritual gifts so that those who possess them work together for the building up of the whole body in love. What comes naturally is the reverse. The gifted compete with one another. They engage in a struggle for power, and their interest is in doing each other down rather than in building each other up.

No church can hope to be effective as a Christian community unless it sees how difficult the achievement of such a community is. Experience throughout the ages, and not least in modern times, suggests that it is not too difficult to establish a reasonably smooth-running community which calls itself a church but which does not cultivate its gifts. This avoids tension but does so at the price of insignificance. It is more difficult, but has proved not to be impossible, to create a quite impressive institution which is controlled through a rigid hierarchy of authority, guiding into predictable channels the will to power of strong individuals, allowing no deviation from the appointed course for the majority, and skillfully forcing spiritually gifted movements which might threaten the position of the hierarchy onto the margins of the institution's life. But any church which tries to grow, to cultivate the best gifts, and to make progress toward the promised maturity in Christ in its common life must recognize from the outset that it is going against the natural grain, and that it needs divine grace to motivate and to purify the will to power of its leaders and its members. That grace is available only through him who commended it to us by dying for us while we were yet sinners.

When Paul said to the Galatians that the fruit or harvest of the Spirit was "love, joy, peace, patience, kindness, goodness, fidelity, gentleness, and self-control," he was not merely piling up a set of admirable qualities in rhetorical fashion. He went on to remind his readers in strong terms that those who belong to Christ Jesus have "crucified the flesh with its passion and desires" (Gal. 5:22–24). By flesh, of course, he meant their ordinary natures in so far as they were not transformed by grace, the grace of the crucified Christ. This prompts Paul to remind them of the dangers of conceit and jealousy. "If a man imagines himself to be somebody, when he is nothing, he is deluding himself" (Gal. 6:3). Life in the Spirit means self-transcendence, and that is peculiarly difficult because it has to be realized in relationship, in close community life where gifts may cut across each other and where vocations may clash. This, again, is why Paul in the same context emphasizes the need for self-criticism and the bearing of one another's burdens (Gal. 6:2).

Christian thinking about church order goes astray when it thinks of that order statically, as settled church communities have always been tempted to do almost throughout their history. No ideal pattern of church order has been bequeathed by the early church which its successors must strive to reproduce exactly in every kind of situation. Such a notion misunderstands the free movement of the Spirit, and if there is anything which the Book of Acts brings out, it is that the church is being truly the church when it detects and responds to that free movement. This is why church order must be dynamic rather than static, an instrument through which the creative power of the Spirit can act. It must therefore be flexible, adaptable, and equipped to be innovative. In this, it is to be contrasted with state order which has to take greater account of the negative elements in power and must, therefore, be more rigid and conservative. It must be even more sharply contrasted with the anarchy into which life slips when people lose their sense of direction and begin to drift. Church order should be the structure of relationships which enables people to keep contact with each other and to maintain continuity with their Christian past while they move forward. This is bound to be complicated because those who follow Christ in the Spirit cannot do so simply by marching in step and certainly not with the predictable shuffle of an ecclesiastical procession.

The gifts of the Spirit are distributed unevenly and often come quite unexpectedly. They demand detours and sudden variations of pace and the alteration of carefully laid plans. Untidy situations are created because, inevitably, some have to move faster than others if they are to be faithful to their vocations. If the Paul who wrote the passage in the letter to the Philippians about pressing toward the mark for the prize of the high calling of God in Christ Jesus (3:14) had been making that point in the passage from Galatians (from which we have already quoted), we can imagine that he might have altered the order in which he named the fruits of the Spirit. "Patience, kindness, goodness, fidelity, gentleness, and self-control" are all necessary if "love, joy, and peace" are to flourish in any community as difficult to handle as the Christian church must be. Otherwise, the "more honorable" members of the body, of whom he speaks in 1 Corinthians 12, will find themselves intolerably frustrated by "the less honorable" and will quickly find what will seem to them to be the best of Christian reasons for moving ahead on their own and leaving the others behind.

This will still be true even if the more gifted make sincere efforts to keep in touch with the less gifted and try to help them, in the spirit of Rom. 15:1 ("We that are strong ought to bear the infirmities of the weak, and not to please ourselves"). Unless they appreciate how difficult this is bound to be, they are likely to make the efforts in the wrong way. They will do so "with the wrong look in their eye," like representatives of colonial powers trying to assist people acutely conscious of their status as subjects and quick to detect and resent any hint of patronage. Gifts always bring power, and a power factor is present even in relations within the body of Christ. It is true here as it is everywhere else that power corrupts. The power must be honestly acknowledged in relations among Christians, and its corruptible possibilities detected, brought out into the open, isolated, and named if there is to be any hope of their being overcome. The more gifted must recognize that they cannot be immune from the temptation of power; they must be particularly suspicious of themselves if they are self-congratulatory about how good their relations with the less powerful are. The less gifted in their turn have to see that their situation also is dangerous. It is as hard to receive benefits without envy or resentment from others more gifted than oneself as it is to confer benefits gracefully. Nor is it any easier to avoid falling into the opposite trap, that of allowing oneself to become unduly dependent on the more gifted and to neglect to make the most of one's own gifts, small though they may be. The very gifts with which the Christian community is endowed to enable it to reach its mark can become the barriers that prevent its doing so. This has severely practical implications for the Christian community today.

8

The Tests of Christian Vocation:
Unity in Tension

ONE OF THE FIRST implications for the Christian community arises in relation to a difficulty which is rarely considered but which often causes a great deal of trouble unless it is frankly recognized from the outset. This is the difficulty which arises in most communities which have a significant public purpose, but one which is likely to be especially acute in the Christian community. The more personal the vocation and the greater the power given for its fulfillment, the greater the disturbance which it is likely to cause. Failure to see this—because of sentimental assumptions that Christian love should simplify and relax relationships rather than deepen and intensify them, while imposing on them the strains which creative action frequently involves—does a great deal of damage. The person with the vocation is caused avoidable frustration and pain, and those around him or her are prevented from responding as positively as they otherwise might.

Although genuine Christian vocation arises within the context of the community and is deeply influenced by the nature of the community, the fact remains that it is usually to the individual that the call first comes. It also comes in an intimately personal way and often leads to a period of isolation in which the exact nature of the vocation has to be defined and a great deal of preparation and reflection takes place. It will frequently mean seeing something which no one else sees initially and trying to make a new departure for which others are not ready and which may provoke resistance even from those on whose cooperation the person with the vocation was counting. The more radical the departure, the greater the resistance is likely to be. Since the Christian community is meant to be composed of pilgrims,

77

striving to move forward and therefore frequently making such new departures, the possibility of strained relationships is one with which it should always be living. Its unity will not be that of passive conformity but one toward which it has to struggle through tension.

Gifted and mature persons with a clear vocation who have pondered on the nature of the ministry of Jesus will recognize from the outset that it is part of the expertise of leadership in the form of a servant to know how to handle this tension. They will be deeply committed, eager to get on with their work, and naturally inclined in the early stages to be impetuous and impatient with those to whom they might reasonably look for support when they prove slow on the uptake or in response. It is precisely at this point that they do well to recall the humility and the careful timing of their Lord. Jesus had far more right to expect understanding and support from his people and had far greater ability to make his meaning clear than even the most devoted and gifted of his followers are ever likely to have. All their vocations will also be far more ambiguous and open to challenge than his. Yet, as we see in the story of his temptations, Jesus found it necessary to spend a great deal of time and effort in examining the various possibilities open to him before he embarked upon his public ministry. Is it likely that those who claim to speak in his name—those who ought to know beyond any doubt how easy it is to claim divine authority for an only too human will to power—should be able to dispense with such a preliminary self-examination? However serious their vocations may be, they fall far short of his. The words "Spare us the test" in the Lord's Prayer are a warning to all of his followers not to suppose that any vocation they have compares with his, especially if they are intoxicated with a sense of the uniqueness of their mission.

It is essential to see this because otherwise charismatic power and the leadership which it should produce is dissipated and can even become destructive. The spiritually gifted must recognize how peculiarly insidious are the temptations to which they are exposed. Few people are disposed to undervalue their vocation or the richness of the gifts with which they have been endowed for its fulfillment. They will usually have good grounds for indignation when others do not respond to them as readily as they should, and they will not lack eloquence in pointing this out. Nothing will be easier than to assume that all the fault for failure lies with the lack of perception of those less gifted than themselves. Scriptural texts will lie conveniently at hand, as they did for Satan in tempting Jesus, to justify this attitude, needing only the slight but fatal movement of identifying their own vocation with that of Jesus and the prophets before him to make them directly applicable. Thus, the modern prophets who are rejected or, even worse, merely ignored, are quick to apply to themselves the ironical words addressed to Isaiah, "Go, and tell this people, 'Hear ye indeed, but understand not; and see ye indeed, but perceive not.' Make the heart of this people fat, and make their ears heavy, and shut their eyes; lest they see with their eyes, and hear with their ears, and understand with their heart, and convert, and be healed" (Isa. 6:9–10, AV) They will find it all the more gratifying to do this when they note that these words are echoed by Jesus himself in explaining why he taught in parables rather than by direct statements (Mark 4:12 and Matt. 13:15).

This temptation is particularly prominent among those who serve churches which have a strong prophetic and critical tradition and which, at the same time, depend on having a broad base of popular support, such as the Protestant churches in English-speaking countries. Many of these churches are composed of the more prosperous members of the communities in which they live, and these churches have inevitably been exposed to the temptations both of complacency and anxiety to preserve the privileged status which prosperity usually brings. Some of their professional ministers are rightly aware of these temptations, but instead of trying to help their people recognize and overcome them, they persuade themselves that their responsibility is discharged by the vehemence with which they denounce their people for being who and where they are—sometimes even giving the impression that they dislike their people so much that the last thing they want is that they should see, hear, understand, convert, and be healed, because that might endanger the professional ministers' own reputations as radical thinkers among their peers. Alternatively, and especially in the United States, with its enormous development of institutions of higher education, they establish themselves on an academic base. From this vantage point they can wax eloquent about the deficiencies of the culture that has produced and sustains them, and they can do this in ways that win ready admiration from the young and inexperienced who are similarly placed. This has the added advantage of minimizing their contact with persons who might be influenced by their prophecy and who might, as a consequence, involve them in the give and take of a relationship among those who share common responsibilities.

If this happens even within the Christian community itself, it is not surprising that it should happen more frequently in the wider society which surrounds it, especially among the numerous heirs of the prophetic Protestant tradition who no longer belong to churches but who are molded by what sociologists call "spilt religion." They have a highly developed critical sense in relation to their environment and, especially, to their own upbringing. But they have little identification with those whom they criticize or, if their criticism becomes sufficiently active to take a political form, even with those, such as the poor and dispossessed, in whose name they claim to speak. They become not the "improving intelligentsia" of Victorian Britain, who consciously strove to place their intelligence at the service of the wider community, but "Superior Persons" who patronize and subtly humiliate those whom they are supposed to serve. They become social irritants rather than reformers, and their potentialities are unrealized. There are many such people in the world of the universities, publishing, broadcasting, and on the fringes of politics in the Anglo-Saxon countries.

The primary interest of those who strive to understand their own vocations in Jesus' light will be in the well-being of those whom they are called to serve, rather than in their own attitude toward them. This will have the effect of diminishing their consciousness of their own originality and, therefore, of their uniqueness. All of us are largely formed by our heritage, even those who imagine themselves to be most radical, and the very tallest cannot see far into the future except on the shoulders of those who have brought them up and gone before them. This is why those who fail to honor their father and their mother are unlikely to provide their children with much that is worthy of honor. More than that, genuine new insight rarely comes except at the frontiers of experience, from beyond rather than within ourselves. It is impossible to reach those frontiers without the help of those who have gone before us and who have shown the way. And once we have arrived, it is impossible to penetrate into the mystery of what lies beyond unless light is given from outside ourselves. Either way, we have cause for humility.

This has two important consequences for the way in which special vocations should be exercised. First, this element of givenness which is present in new insight must be reflected in the way in which the insight is passed on to others. If a hand has been stretched out to pull forward those with the special vocation when they were at the limit of their own capacity, then they must put out their own hands in order to help others. Any valid insight is likely to be given for the sake of others as well as themselves, and it carries with it a responsibility to pass it on in the most useful way possible. Those to whom it has to be passed on may well be further back, clumsier, less committed, and more inexperienced, but they have not heard the same call and will lack some of the gifts which the call brings with it. The rule has to be that the more important and genuinely original the insight is, the more essential it becomes to show patience and perseverance in conveying it to others. Those who save inexperienced climbers stranded on a ledge do not walk away in disgust because those in distress were fools to have gotten into difficulties in the first place, or because they are incompetent in handling a rope, or because they are more concerned for their own safety than for the dangers to which they are exposing their rescuers, or because they give way to panic. The more a genuine vocation works itself out in the life of the community, the heavier the responsibility becomes for its possessor to help others to share in it.

This is reinforced by the other consequence. While a particular vocation is likely to arise in loneliness and must be true to itself and not compromise its distinctiveness in order to win quick approval from others, it nearly always needs to be complemented by the activities of others with different vocations and different gifts. As we have already reminded ourselves, Paul's teaching about the mutual dependence of the members of Christ's body arose precisely in relation to problems that tore apart the exceptionally "gifted" church at Corinth, where gifts clashed and where the richly endowed were quick to look down on those who were not, apparently even in the context of the Lord's Supper itself. This again finds confirmation on other, more mundane levels of experience. The coach of a sports team knows how important it is not only to have a balanced set of abilities among the players but also an attitude among them which ensures that each plays to the strong points of the others and covers up for their weaknesses. The casualty rate among football and soccer coaches suggests that this is more easily said than done even in sports. It is certainly not less difficult to do in more significant spheres. Competition and even a measure of rivalry may have their strictly delimited place within the Christian community, but they are not appropriate on levels where people are meant to be working together toward a common goal. Yet it is only too familiar a fact that "interservice rivalry"—a revealingly self-contradictory phrase—is not confined to the armed forces alone. It is found in the civil and social services, in the academic world, and not least, in the churches themselves. Eleven o'clock on Sunday morning is the time when rivalry in the service of the one God who insists that the gifts of the Spirit are provided for the building up of the whole body in love is most acute and most shameless.

The damage done by this inappropriate rivalry can hardly be exaggerated, not least in situations where it is so taken for granted that people are unaware that anything is amiss. To take one instance from the internal life of the Christian community—those gifted and trained in theology, especially if they serve in academic institutions, are sometimes so conscious of their superior enlightenment to those who may be less well trained, whose gifts may be different, and who serve ordinary congregations that they make little effort to communicate with them. They devote most of their energies instead to writing and speaking for their professional colleagues, sometimes even allowing their own students only to overhear their conversation on their own terms. In their turn, those who minister to ordinary congregations in very unacademic contexts resent the attitude of professional theologians and are irritated by the apparent irrelevance of their works to the situations which have to be addressed. Their tendency, therefore, is to ignore the theologians and to make no effort to communicate with them, priding themselves by contrast on their own down-to-earth practicality. In consequence, there is no interchange of gifts and both parties are impoverished. The professional theologians work on the basis of too abstract a knowledge of common human experience and are in danger of becoming insensitive to the way in which issues with which they themselves have to be concerned actually arise in the untidy circumstances of daily life. The "working ministers" fail to make the necessary efforts to appropriate the insights of the theologians for themselves and are unable to pass them on in an assimilable form to those among whom they work. Thus, the gifted fail to exercise their vocation aright, and the hungry sheep look up and are not fed.

If two such groups in the church with closely related and mutually dependent gifts fail to set an example, it is hardly surprising that interservice and interunion rivalries should do so much to bedevil professional and industrial life. The social consequences of these often become quickly visible through strikes and public controversies. There are other more pervasive failures whose consequences are less obvious but no less damaging. The recent enormous expansion of higher education has meant that those who have been highly educated are now much more numerous and touch the rest of the community at more points than ever before. This has not increased their ability to share their gifts and the fruits of their education with those who have not been educated in the same way. If their education has been truly successful, it should equip them to be sensitive in appreciating the qualities of those who lack their skill in dealing with abstract ideas in formalized ways, so that they can be more effective in communicating with them. Sometimes, however, it seems to make them more insensitive and more impatient toward those who do not quickly grasp what they are saying in their own terms. This has two evil consequences. It denies to the less well educated much of what the more highly educated have to offer them. It also prevents the latter from acknowledging the extent to which they and the rest of society depend for their own effectiveness on the proper exercise of their own gifts by the former. Those, when they are gifted, often possess not only essential manual, technical, or artistic skills, but they also have a warmth, directness, and sense of what belongs to our common humanity which are at least as vital to the health of a society increasingly dominated by elaborate technology and administration as more specialized forms of expertise.

In *The Educated Society*,[1] written when the great expansion of higher education in the sixties was just beginning, I called attention to the danger of a new class distinction emerging in Western society between those who have elaborate formal education and those who do not. This danger has been largely realized, and its consequences have been less serious than they might have been only because of the incompetence shown by many of the highly educated in taking advantage of their social privileges. Such people have often shown themselves to be lacking in stability and balance—in other words, in common sense—and have proved vulnerable to that childish trendiness which, as Ephesians 4 reminds us, is the characteristic weakness of those who misuse their gifts. Their less gifted neighbors who rely more on tradition, convention, and folk memory, and through these have learned the value of communal loyalty and mutual trust, often show themselves to be more deeply rooted and, therefore, less easily swayed. This is not to imply that right is necessarily always on their side. Their obvious danger is that they might settle into complacency and the kind of sloth which makes them resist change, especially the kind of change which is produced by new ideas. They need the gifted as much as the gifted need them, which makes it so important that there should be effective communication between them.

The New Testament says that, although Jesus had compassion on the multitudes, seeing them as sheep without a shepherd, he still insisted that salvation consisted for them, as for everyone else, in being called out of the multitudes by name for a particular and personal vocation. He demanded of everyone whom he called a measure of seriousness which reflected the seriousness of his own vocation. In the apostolic community, under the guidance of his Spirit, the same seriousness and personal dignity are to be shown with the recognition that all gifts, greater and lesser, are necessary for the achievement of maturity for the whole body. Churches have a special responsibility in these days to create a community in which the more and the less gifted can build each other up, making the most of their differing powers. They are less exposed to the temptations of intellectual pride than academic communities, they have a much more mixed membership, and in these days their service offers fewer glittering prizes than does the service of the world. The fulfillment of this responsibility is not the least important part of their reconciling and healing work.

9

Men, Women, and Maturity

CHRISTIAN MATURITY has to be expressed in all parts of life, and this is true of intimate personal relations no less than of the general life of the church. In some ways, its nature should be most clearly visible here because our actions are more directly under our own control and the problems inherent in the existence of all institutions less obtrusive. Yet, just because we are so involved personally, it is here also that the difficulties can be at their most acute.

We will consider first a matter which is of almost obsessive preoccupation in Western countries today, that of relations between men and women. That the preoccupation has this obsessive quality is one of the signs that the times are out of joint. This condition will not be removed until the Christian community has shown more imaginative insight into the subject than it has so far been able to find.

This is not to imply that all elements in the preoccupation are unhealthy. It has arisen partly as a consequence of the greatly enhanced self-consciousness and sense of individuality which have long been characteristics of the modern world but to which women have only recently taken the opportunity to give expression as well as men. In this situation, we are fortunate in having a classic Christian statement of what this individuality means, one which takes the measure of what it involves. Admittedly, it is written by a man, but by a man who, as we shall see, had the deepest respect for this individuality in women also.

Søren Kierkegaard believed that it was his vocation to work out as fully as possible what it means to be the self-conscious individual before God, as seriously as Descartes did but with a more active awareness of what God's providential rule means and always with the knowledge that individuality has ultimately to find its fulfillment in community, in the realization of the universal human.[1] It is in this context that we must consider the significance of his action in breaking his engagement to marry Regine Olsen, the young girl whom he loved and who loved him. The banal reductionism of those who try to explain it away on the basis of some physical or psychic defect can be dismissed out of hand by anyone who has taken the trouble to read anything Kierkegaard wrote about personal relationships. We can safely take it that he meant what he said when he related it to his vocation to explore what it means to be the individual and that he lacked confidence that both he and Regine possessed the spiritual resources to maintain that vocation in the married state. "If I had had enough faith, I would have remained with Regine." It was evidence of his fundamental maturity, of his recognition that full humanity is cohumanity. He knew that his destiny was to realize the universal human and that it was the aim of the reflective person to achieve maturity on a profounder level than is possible without reflection, but he was afraid that he could not trust himself to maintain the tension involved in faithfulness to his vocation unless he could rely on the understanding cooperation of his partner.

It was not that he was worried that he and Regine would not be happy together but that they would find happiness too readily on a superficial level and forget their vocation. His nightmare was that they might end up like Frederic and Juliana, the complacently domesticated couple in their cozy country parsonage whom he satirized with increasing bitterness as he grew older. It is a pity that we never had Regine's side of the story, expressed with something approaching the self-consciousness and power of articulation of Søren. We might have learned something of the way in which those who have a highly developed sense of individuality and those who have the gift of achieving spontaneity more simply and directly, without having to make herculean creative efforts to get themselves out of the way, can complement each other and build each other up. And if they had been able to marry, Søren, with his incomparable genius, might have been able to give us that account of the true inwardness of the marriage relationship which the Christian community badly needs in these confused and unhappy times. He might also have given us that fresh light on how to bring up the children of the covenant, upon whom the burden of individuality lies so heavily, which we need hardly less badly. It was not to be and, in this slackly hedonistic age, we are left only to admire the superb restraint and tenderness which Søren showed in resisting the temptation to have less than a full marriage in the way he understood it with the Regine he dearly loved, for her sake as much as his own. He was no Byron or Wagner, and he spared Regine the kind of tortured Scandinavian marriage which Ibsen or Ingmar Bergmann would have loved to delineate.

We have to do without Kierkegaard's celebration of the relationship between man and woman, therefore, but we do, at least, have Karl Barth's extensive treatment of the subject.[2] This lacks the concentration, the wit, and the elegance of style of Kierkegaard, its exegesis of the second creation story in Genesis is more free than modern scholarship will allow, and there is one important place where I should want to put the emphasis very differently. But Barth's treatment has the merit of discussing the subject in the context of Christian maturity, and it makes some fundamental points with great clarity.

The first of these is his insistence that humanity is cohumanity. On the face of it, that might seem to be so obvious in this context as not to be worth saying. That "man is for the woman made and the woman for the man," in the words of the old song, is hardly an original insight. Yet because our estrangement from ourselves means the distortion of relationships on the most basic levels, it is here that things begin to go most wrong, and Barth brings this out very clearly by his imaginative treatment of the second creation story. The damage goes right back to the roots, and true radicalism means a reexamination of the roots. And being so deep-rooted, this is the hardest relationship to set right. Barth's point is that to see that humanity is cohumanity is an insight which, in our fallen state, we can only properly apprehend by grace coming from outside ourselves.

It is not surprising, therefore, that most of the temptations of success which afflict the Christian life are as active in relations between men and women in their distinctiveness as anywhere else, and that they need the presence of all the virtues of maturity if they are to be overcome. Even in Christian circles, people have become so preoccupied with the sexual aspects of this relationship that its other temptations and its other hopeful possibilities have not received sufficient attention. The sexual aspect cannot, of course, be overlooked—as though there were any danger of that happening in these days—but many sexual problems are intensified because attitudes are wrong on other levels. Most of us have to get ourselves out of the way before we can discover each other and, in the process, our common maturity; and the more self-conscious we are, the more this matters. It is another strength of Barth's discussion that he says that the main Christian argument in favor of monogamy is that it brings out most clearly the commitment involved in uniquely and honestly personal choice. It is the best human analogy to the way in which God has chosen us. This is the place on earth where liberation, as the Christian understands it, finds its best expression—in an act of responsible choice that inevitably carries with it an explicit limitation in other directions if the reciprocity which is integral to the relationship is to be achieved.

The great objection to notions of free love, which have a recurring fascination for some Christian heretics and which are having one of their periodic revivals today, is that they fail to do justice to the way in which freedom has to express itself in this context. The degree of commitment which the relationship demands from both parties is such that all the spiritual resources available for this aspect of their lives are needed for its fulfillment. It may, perhaps, be theoretically possible for more than two people to have such a relationship with each other simultaneously, but the possibilities of mutual and self-deception are so infinite and the vulnerability of the partners to being wounded by each other so great that a measure of sanctity would be required on all sides for which most of us have to wait until the world to come where, we are reliably informed, there is neither marrying nor giving in marriage. The very limitation involved in the act of commitment in marriage is itself part of the paradigm of how freedom works in cohumanity.[3] It does this not least because experience proves that it gives that release from self-preoccupation which enables those who accept it to act with a new kind of detached goodwill to others. It is those who know marriage in this way who find it easiest to be of gentle spirit, peacemakers, generous, magnanimous, and joyful, although it is also true that, as we might expect, they also find it easier to succumb to pride, complacency, and sloth.

In the *Dogmatics* Barth is open to criticism at a surprising place, given his characteristic emphasis in theology and all the remarkable insights he has to offer about the nature of time. He does not see the relationship between men and women sufficiently in an eschatological context. This may be partly because, in the way he chose to make his exposition unfold, he dealt with ethics so extensively under the heading of the doctrine of creation,[4] but it has a regrettable consequence. Because he concentrates so much on the Genesis story, remarkably positive as his interpretation of it may be, he has to give undue weight to the notions of masculine precedence and feminine subordination. Paul before him had to do the same, but with more excuse. The Genesis story may faithfully reflect the way in which we have evolved, but even when it is given the Christian interpretation Barth provides, it remains an account of what is past.[5] And as Barth himself would be among the first to insist, it is what lies ahead which matters most for the follower of Christ. The nature of our cohumanity is not determined by the creation story but by what we know of God in Christ, and Christ is more than what is recorded for us of the man Jesus. He is the exalted Christ, who now calls us forward in the Spirit. To quote 1 John: "Beloved, we are God's children now; it does not yet appear what we shall be, but we know that when he appears we shall be like him, for we shall see him as he is."[6] The pointers which the Spirit gives concerning the nature of that life emphasizes its equality and mutuality,[7] and this should determine our relationships here and now, rather than any orders of precedence which are projected forward from past experience and whose relevance diminishes the more we move forward in our new life.

What implications does this have? First, because men and women have a common calling as children of God, with all the concomitants for maturity which we have tried to see, especially in relation to freedom, choice, and responsibility, it is not at this fundamental level that any differences between men and women can have significance. As Barth himself says, any attempt to differentiate masculine and feminine principles at this level can be nothing other than dangerously misleading. Those women who fight to maintain the recognition in practice of the principle that this freedom is inherent in our humanity and not the prerogative of the members of one sex are fighting the battle of all, and it is a matter of deep shame to the Christian community that it has so often to be fought on Christian soil. Humanity is cohumanity. We are ourselves only in relationship, and all are impoverished if the full freedom and responsibility of some are denied. This is especially true of the most fundamental of relationships.

Second, this common calling does not remove the differences between men and women any more for that matter than it removes the differences among members of the same sex, but it does determine the way in which they are to be dealt with. As Barth finely puts it, the differences prompt us to consider one another, hear the question which each puts to the other, and make responsible answer to one another.[8] We cannot ignore the differences. We are unsettled by them, so that there is an inescapable tension in our dealings with each other. They pose the question concerning our humanity as we meet it in a different form from that which we know in ourselves, although Barth does not discuss the problem of the exact way in which this question differs when it concerns the relationship between men and women from when it concerns any relationship with another person. Where he comes near to doing so, he is likely to arouse a good deal of controversy in these days because he maintains the traditional position that the relationship between men and women is controlled by a definite order, in which man precedes woman.

In saying this, Barth shows uncharacteristic concern to safeguard himself against misunderstanding. He does not want this to be taken in any crudely male chauvinist way, and he is at pains to emphasize that the mutuality of the relationship must be understood in a fully Christian sense. "Man speaks against himself," he says in his earlier treatment of the same theme, "if he assesses and treats woman as an inferior being for without her weakness and subsequence he would not be man. And woman speaks against herself if she envies that which is proper to man, for his strength and precedence are the reality without which she could not be woman."[9] In fairness to Barth, that quotation with its references to weakness and subsequence may be misleading. He himself issues a warning against giving theological weight to secondary male and female characteristics which are relative, historically conditioned, and stand in need of constant critical scrutiny. We can be confident that despite his Swiss citizenship he would have been on the side of campaigners for women's rights on many of the issues for which they fight. The question remains, however, as to how far it is appropriate any longer to think of relations between men and women in terms of strength, weakness, precedence, and subsequence, let alone of superiority and inferiority. And by "any longer" I do not refer to the second half of the twentieth century, as though any special insight has been given to us and denied to our forebears. I refer to the Christian dispensation as a whole, where what we are to become, not what we have been, must be determinative. With all its limitations, the Pauline teaching about relations between men and women, like the practice of Jesus, represented an advance on current practice of the time. The question is whether we have continued to make the progress inherent in the basic insights of our faith or whether we have fallen back.

This is a large matter, and it would be foolish to rush in with a conclusion, especially as the atmosphere of the present time is not conducive to taking cool looks at this subject in a long perspective. Let me simply say this, which will, I hope, be taken as evidence of my good faith in relation to the fundamental equality of men and women in cohumanity. We shall be in a better position to evaluate what truth, error, and continuing relevance for the present situation there is in the admittedly biblical notion of masculine precedence when we have an analysis of the notion by a woman theologian that shows an insight and grasp of first principles at least comparable to that of Barth.[10] It should be added that masculine theologians stand in need of such a study as much as women do for the sake of their competence at their own jobs, because without it they will not define cohumanity in this sphere aright and will have to face the possibility that they may have a large number of words to eat. Until such a work appears, no theological judgments should be made which assume the self-evident truth of this notion because it is found in Scripture and tradition.

Third, and related to this, there is no other subject than this where it is more appropriate and more important that the Christian community should conduct its discussion according to its own highest standards of civility. Obstinate masculine conservatism and militant feminism are equally out of place, although there may be more excuse for the latter than the former. Here, above all, the virtues of maturity should be receiving their clearest expression, the gentleness of spirit which expresses itself in tenderness and readiness to listen, the peacemaking without which a true home cannot come into being, generosity which puts the most positive interpretation on the difficulties and aspirations of the other, the magnanimity which is tolerant and forgiving when people believe that they have been wounded by sexual discrimination, and above all joy. Insofar as women succeed in expressing more fully the liberation which is already our common possession in Christ, this should be an occasion for celebration, to men as well as to themselves. Since humanity is cohumanity, we shall all be enriched by it.[11] Surely in these matters above all others it is the denial of our faith to treat each other as opponents, and we do not have to speak of them to each other as though we were foreigners, those of strange tongue, and not fellow members of the house of Israel.

This becomes the more important to remember when we realize that if there are to be changes in the respective roles of men and women in the family and in the wider life of society, this demands greater understanding and mutual respect between them, not less. If, for example, a woman wishes to start or to renew a career in middle life after concentrating for many years on her home and children, this imposes a fresh strain both upon her and her husband at a time when marriages are in any case often vulnerable. Here, as elsewhere, relationships need to deepen as their range grows. Christians in these days are, of course, much disturbed by the problems created by marital breakdown, increasingly within the heart of the Christian community itself, but we have still not paid enough attention to what maturity in marriage involves, nor set our sights high enough for what we might expect successful lifelong marriage to achieve, nor drawn sufficiently on the resources which are available to help toward its fulfillment by overcoming pride, complacency, and sloth.

This may also help to reestablish or, where necessary, to create civilized conventions of behavior in other relationships than those of marriage. Here also the temptations as well as the virtues of maturity need to be borne particularly in mind, because we are easily able to deceive each other and sometimes ourselves. This is obviously and especially true in relations between men and women who have not reached the point of marital commitment. One of the marks of a mature Christian community should be that it has well-defined and yet subtle and sensitive courting conventions, which try to safeguard the seriousness and the mystery of commitment by providing people with plenty of opportunities to deepen their knowledge of each other while, at the same time, laying emphasis on the restraint which is a barrier to exploitation and allowing ways of graceful withdrawal without causing avoidable wounds. We have served our children ill in this generation by not fighting harder to retain what seemly conventions existed in this area, leaving them to work out conventions of their own in a cruel world, where the cynical standards of commercial hucksters reign or where they have little protection against the harsh conformisms of their shortsighted peer groups in college or apartment land.

High standards and clear conventions over marriage and what leads up to it will also help restore civility to other relationships which have suffered impoverishment. This is particularly true of friendship, where excessive self-consciousness about the sexual element, which might be one factor among others in it, has made people nervous and inhibited. One of the advantages of the rigidity of convention in relation to marriage and sexual expression which prevailed in Christian circles in Victorian times, uncharitably as it may sometimes have been maintained, was that it liberated people to show the warmth of affection in other relationships of life, toward relatives, children, and friends of either sex without the fear of being misunderstood. Christians should show indignation at the way in which literary busybodies grub away at the details of private lives of our forebears in the hope of finding some dirt in a corner, which they then proudly display before the gaze of every passer-by, meanwhile protesting that, of course, from their enlightened point of view, it is not dirt. Maturity should give us the confidence not to be deterred by the pseudotolerance of the prurient from expressing healthy natural affection in ways appropriate to the level of commitment involved in the relationship. It is an impoverished society indeed where friends and colleagues, whether of the same or the other sex, are embarrassed about being seen much in each other's company because of what people might say, or where only the potential dangers and none of the beauty of the love of bachelors and spinsters for young children are dwelt upon. It is not Lewis Carroll but those who write about him in such terms who see anything sinister in the affectionately humorous and utterly unsentimental observation which he bestows on Alice. Victorian standards were far from ideal, and they were often severely damaged by undue class consciousness, but the very zeal with which their limitations and hypocrisies have been documented by their successors suggests that all has not been progress since their time. Quite apart from what is happening in the world around us, a new effort to set itself higher standards of maturity in these matters is required by the Christian community itself.

10

Youth, Age, and Faith

THE OBSERVATIONS just made about the Victorians have a measure of truth also in the sphere of relationships between parents and children and, more broadly, between age and youth. The typical Victorians saw clearly enough the need to train their children in the acceptance of responsibility and also realized the importance of passing on the best of their own experience, by precept and example supported by strong conventions. They saw life, as all mature societies must, in a perspective longer than that of one generation. What many of them did not see so clearly was how success and the power it brings can corrupt even the most high-minded, nor did they readily appreciate the problems which arise for the children of the successful if they are to arrive at their own maturity.

The story of Abraham and Isaac has already been referred to, and I have always regarded it as one of the confirmations of the divine inspiration of Scripture that it emerged from the mists of antiquity at the very beginning of the history of Israel. The point is missed unless we see that Abraham's trial befell him in order to warn him of the dangers of success. He is the archetype of the rich man, the one blessed by God, and it is in Isaac, through whom alone the covenant promise is to be fulfilled, that all his riches are concentrated. Some aspects of the significance of the demand that Abraham sacrifice Isaac for the church's understanding of its vocation have already been discussed. It is no less significant for relations within the natural family. For Abraham to have set his love of Isaac above God would have been to stunt Isaac, making him over into Abraham's image and thus preventing him from achieving his own maturity, turning him into the conservative described in our third chapter. It is only when Abraham has achieved the inner detachment which makes him see that he must not get in the way of Isaac's own relation with God that he becomes fit to be entrusted with Isaac's upbringing.

Isaac remains the heir and has to carry on the tradition, but Abraham can prepare him for this without falling into the error of either paternalism or maternalism, if these slightly dubious metaphorical terms are not entirely inappropriate. The danger of the former, which was particularly acute in Victorian Britain, is that the child will be kept too long in a subordinate position. The child is given the advantage of a disciplined upbringing and is trained to expect to make its own judgments and carry responsibility, but the father may be so anxious that the child should follow in his own footsteps and may be so sure that he knows best that the child is denied the necessary freedom. But if paternalism is the characteristic danger of successful old-established societies, families, and businesses, maternalism is that of successful new ones, as well as of those which are reacting against the excessive paternalism of their own parents. The parents will have worked so hard for success in their own terms that they have little time and imagination left with which to enjoy it. They want to enjoy success through their children. The result is that, as we say, they "spoil" them, while at the same time laying the burden of great expectations upon them. Not only must they carry on the success of their parents but their success, in ways the parents can enjoy, must be more spectacular, since through the efforts of their parents they have so many more advantages. Yet to the extent that they have been "spoiled," they lack the training to reach their own maturity. If, nevertheless, they manage to do so, it will be in ways which disconcert and disappoint their parents. Either way, as recent experience in much of Western society proves, mutual misunderstanding and frustration are likely to follow and an unhealthily large "gap" between the generations emerges.

An English sociologist, Frank Musgrove, wrote a book in the early sixties called *Youth and the Social Order,* in which he argued that higher education was a conspiracy to mold young people to fulfill a subordinate role for as long as possible and keep them out of competition with their elders. It was a development of the concept of adolescence,[1] which was invented for that very reason approximately the same time as the steam engine, with all the new social implications that industrialization brought. This is a tendentious half-truth.[2] Adolescence is also a consequence of a more developed sense of increased individuality and education, and the period of study, reflection, and controlled irresponsibility which it provides is an invaluable aid in reaching independence of judgment and a higher level of maturity than would otherwise be possible in an increasingly complex society. Yet this half-truth has the merit of shaking the complacency of the academic community, with its characteristic assumption that the kind of higher education it offers is always self-evidently a good thing and its tendency to ignore the extent of its dependence on attitudes taken for granted in the wider community to which it belongs. When people in that wider community no longer possess strong convictions of their own and allow the next generation to work out its own salvation, soothing their consciences by making available to it the resources of higher education while retaining real power for themselves, many of the conditions for the creation of an alienated generation are present. The leaders of the academic community, by the policy of heedless expansion without reference to wider social considerations which they have pursued in several Western lands over the last generation, cannot escape some of the responsibility for the creation of such conditions.

In another recent book, *Saeculum: History and Society in the Theology of St. Augustine,*[3] R. A. Markus helps us to see the relation between youth and age in a different perspective. He points out that when the ancients wanted an example of weakness, they took it not from age but from youth. Weak adults produce vulnerable children, and they realized that children are particularly exposed to contagious diseases. The longer they are kept as children, *in statu pupillari,* the more virulent the disease becomes, just as measles and chicken pox are more damaging in late youth than in early childhood. All this suggests that, instead of echoing the noisiest cries of pain of those who are suffering in these ways or of providing them only with tea and sympathy, Christians concerned with growth toward maturity would be better employed in asking whether we have gotten the balance and the timing between minority and majority right. All institutions become possessive and like to keep their children in the nest for too long. We shall see that this is true of churches. It may be that this is now more urgently true of institutions of higher education. They are unlikely to find a satisfactory answer unless they are submitted to unwelcome pressure from outside themselves.

Real freedom for those who live after us means the ability to look into the unknown for themselves and there make their own decisions. Success for their parents comes only when they are able to do so on their parent's shoulders, seeing further than they would have been able to do without their help. If those who carry the burdens of maturity find that they are unable to walk upright as they do so,[4] the range of the vision of their children will inevitably be narrowed. The difficulties which many of the most apparently privileged young people in the Western world experience today suggest that the fault may well lie as much with the immaturity of their parents as with their own.

If our immaturity is causing problems to our children, it may also be building up difficulties for ourselves and for our immediate predecessors as we move into old age. The next group that is likely to be the victim of the uncertainty and confused guilt feelings of the liberally minded is the aged. This has already begun to happen in Britain. As with all groups who suffer this fate, the aged do so because, in relation to them, those who should be acting in a mature way have a great deal about which to feel guilty. Many of them have lost the perspective on life which enables them to give dignity to old age, and their hedonism can find no place for those who cannot contribute to their pleasure or even fend for themselves. Yet, as with prematurity, even efforts to redress this situation can make it worse if an inadequate response to the challenge of maturity leads people to a wrong conception of what postmaturity should be like, speaking of postmaturity here in relation to the natural life cycle.

The danger is that, in compensation for past failures, old people are encouraged to become primarily the recipients of charity and thus overdependent, with the consequence that their own maturity is diminished and the advent of second childhood is hastened. Here above all, we need to beware of Christians when they come bearing gifts. Those who, like myself, are themselves drawing near to old age should take the initiative while there is still time to work out a different approach.

First, as they grow older they should organize their lives so as to ensure that they remain active and useful as long as possible, while at the same time continuing to be aware that the virtues and the temptations of maturity can still be present. It is vital that the inner detachment be maintained which enables them to see that the worst way to keep useful as well as active is by clinging to responsibility and power which are now more appropriately exercised by others. Continuing maturity is best demonstrated by the voluntary surrender of these before the point is reached when their possessors themselves feel that they are becoming too much for them. This is unlikely to become clear to them before it is clear to their colleagues. They should also have the good sense to know that, if they are to undertake new responsibilities, more suited to advancing years and declining powers, they will need all the energy they still feel for making the necessary adjustments and starting their new tasks with zest. People are likely to be more effective in their sixties if they stop going on trying increasingly hard to do what was appropriate for them in their forties or fifties, and they are probably able to continue to be useful for much longer.

Second, it matters a great deal that these changes be made with due respect for the dignity of old age. This is more than a matter of softening the impact of painful change, although since we shall all have to go this way one day we have a common interest in doing this. It is one of creating the conditions in which older people can make their best contribution. The graceful phasing out from responsibility should be as high an art in a civilized community as the phasing into it over which we seem to have such difficulty today. The prophet speaks of the young having visions and the old dreaming dreams. Visions refer to as yet unrealized possibilities, dreams to illuminating reorganizations of past experience. As the young mature and try to implement their visions, the old can provide correctives and amendments to their efforts and do so without, however, having the power and responsibility to carry them through, which would mean the inevitable distortion of the vision. It is the practice in Britain to elevate superannuated politicians and other public servants to the House of Lords, where much of what they do is exactly that. The excessive archaism and pomp of the House of Lords do not commend it as a model, but its function might be more widely copied, as it has been in the Canadian senate. It would be easiest to start with professional groups which have a good deal of freedom to reorganize themselves along these lines.[5] This might help throw light on how to approach the much more difficult problems of those who face old age with little formal education and with skills diminishing rapidly because they are based on physical capacity. One of the insufficiently considered costs of our overindustrialized and overmechanized society is that old age is much harder to bear than it used to be in traditional society for those who have had to carry some of its heaviest burdens. The freedom to watch television is a poor substitute for freedom from loneliness and loss of function.

Three considerations should govern a Christian approach to this matter. First, the importance of building up resources in order to meet the demands of postmaturity while we still have the strength of maturity must be emphasized. This means more than the sensible cultivation of interests and hobbies which can be carried through into retirement. It is a matter of the way in which one spends one's whole life, so that one has a fund of memories and generous reflections which can sustain one's spirit in solitude and sleeplessness or illness. Since the memories of childhood seem to recur with special vividness in old age, a rich childhood has special importance. One of the sad things about many people today as they face old age is the poverty of their inner life in youth and maturity. The fact that most of us live longer than our forebears did means that our earlier development should be fuller and stronger. It is not always evident that this is so.

Second, the support of the wider community is, if anything, even more necessary in old age than earlier, not merely for material help but also for giving the stimulus to continuing activity. It is a common complaint, especially in an old country like Britain, that the churches fail to capture the loyalty of the young. This is understandable, but it sometimes prevents us from seeing that the old also need evangelism. This is not necessarily because, as they near their journey's end, people become more interested in what lies beyond than in the passing scene. Observation suggests that it is usually only those who have been alive to that question at other stages in their journey who are able to raise it with enough existential intensity to hope to receive any fresh answers at a time when their imagination and critical faculties are in decline, although bereavement may sometimes bestir them. It is rather that people need to be called out of their isolation and gathered into a community which serves a purpose greater than their own as much when they are old, when it is so easy to slip into self-centered isolation, as when they are younger. Any service they do must be realistically related to their capacities and sensitively linked with what those coming after them are doing, and this demands unsentimental honesty and frankness on both sides, but there is no reason why it should not be genuinely creative. It could be that in the period which succeeds that of Christendom, if ours is indeed a post-Christendom age, it would be to the old rather than to the young that one would look most hopefully for guidance. When the world is tired and vision seems to have faded, those with the longest memories and the fullest experience of life may be better able to draw on the wisdom of the past to help in the present. And those few who have maintained their vigilance with such alertness that, as they draw near to it, they could have fresh insight into eternity, may also be able to tell us what matters most about the future.

Third, it follows from this that there must be much more interchange among people at the various stages of life than is customary in modern society. The rule that we all need each other, and the best of each other, holds throughout the whole of life. Obviously the old, like everyone else, need institutions and facilities that cater to their special needs, and this is particularly true of the very old and the handicapped. And we have already emphasized that they will be scrupulous, even to the point of being overscrupulous, not to get in the way and therefore in the light of those who are younger. But there must be relationship as well as differentiation, and the whole community suffers when there is disproportionate segregation. The young need to see people aging with dignity and gathering the fruits in their lives of an earlier period than their own. They also need to be reminded of dissolution and death, and of the need to come to terms with bereavement. And, as we have said, the old need, in due but not excessive measure, the stimulus of the fresh approach to life of the young. Humanity is cohumanity, and that is true among people at life's various stages as well as between men and women. When only one stage of life is taken into account and regarded as the norm, all is distorted. Christian maturity enables us to act our age, at whatever stage of the natural cycle we may happen to be, but it does so only by teaching us how much we depend upon each other, right through. When it does, it can provide us with some of life's most satisfying experiences. For an old person to pretend to act like a young one is unseemly, but nothing is more beautiful than to see old people stimulated by the young into a vitality which enables them to handle the possibilities of their present situation in such a way as to give the young a glimpse of what they must have been like in their youth. Nothing, that is, unless it is for the old to see emerging in the young the promise of a coming maturity which is gentle, peaceful, generous, magnanimous, and joyful in its strength.

Work and Play

COMPARATIVELY LITTLE attention has been paid to the subject of work in the history of Protestant theology. It is true that the World Council of Churches promoted some studies of the subject under the heading of "The Responsible Society" after the war, and there has been some treatment of it with particular reference to industry in books dealing with industrial mission,[1] but these are recent and not very extensive. The so-called Protestant ethic, which is supposed to be an ethic of work, has been much discussed; but it was the discovery of Max Weber, a speculative German sociologist with little direct knowledge of the Anglo-Saxon countries from which he drew most of his material. The ethic has, in fact, received more attention from sociologists, literary critics, and publicists celebrating or lamenting its alleged decline than from theologians and church historians. Sermons and popular Protestant literature, especially in Britain and the USA in the late nineteenth and early twentieth centuries, emphasized the virtues of honesty, diligence, punctuality, thrift, and self-improvement. But this could have been as much a response to the social needs of the time as the result of anything inherent in Protestant theology and ethos. It may be significant that in his book, *The Religious Factor*,[2] which was based on a study of old-established ethnic groups in Detroit, Gerhardt Lenski was able to show that actively practicing Catholics exemplified the "Protestant ethic" almost as clearly as their Protestant counterparts. It was nonpracticing Catholics who contrived to maintain, even in an American context, the more relaxed attitude toward work supposedly characteristic of Catholic culture, especially in peasant societies.

This may be a warning against accepting popular generalizations too readily, even when they come wearing academic dress, but it also underlines how much the matter needs more attention from Protestant theology. Such attention has tended to oscillate between uncritical acceptance of assumptions about work current in the milieu in which it is most accustomed to operate, which are those of what is called the "Protestant ethic," and, on the other hand, a romantic idealism which protests against the inequalities and inhumanities of existing economic orders. So far as Protestant theology has been influenced by Marxist analysis, it has generally been more preoccupied with its wider social and political implications than with its direct influence on work situations.[3]

This is regrettable because Protestant theology has much to contribute to a Christian understanding of maturity in relation to work. Barth's treatment of the subject, which is itself largely neglected,[4] makes this clear with refreshingly down-to-earth practicality. Work, he says, is necessary for the preservation, safeguarding, and fashioning of human life. It has to be carried out objectively, honestly, and cooperatively. Stated thus summarily, this may sound abstract rather than down-to-earth, but he specifies in some detail what he means by these, and his treatment has the merit of setting work free from the demonic character which so often belongs to it in the modern world. What Barth is saying, in effect, is that work is there, it has to be done, and humankind must get on with it with the minimum of fuss. Yet work must not simply be taken for granted. It is limited by other factors which deserve attention. It is not an automatic but a *human* activity, with self-awareness and appreciation of the struggle involved in overcoming intractable material.[5]

Barth also has practical things to say about the relation between work and vocation. Even when one's work is one's vocation, it is important to distinguish the two, just as it is essential to distinguish the function of the state from that of the church even when the state is composed of committed Christians. Thus, he says, preachers should take pride in being good at their craft, and their lofty vocation, so far from enabling them to forget this, should lay this obligation upon them all the more firmly. Barth relates how much more satisfactory he found a well-performed variety act he saw one Saturday evening than the bumblingly incompetent sermon he had to sit through on the following Sunday morning, and most of us would readily agree with him. Yet unlike that of a vocation, the work commitment is a limited one. It is right to ask questions about work such as, "Is it necessary? Could I be more usefully employed?" These are obviously questions which have to be asked with increasing pertinence in the modern world.

This is valuable as far as it goes, but even granting that the professional theologian cannot claim expertise on all aspects of work, is it enough? Though work may still reflect the curse of Adam, it can also be creative, and as such it also has to face the problems of success. And this is true not only of vocational work, as in the case of creative artists, but of everyday work also. For example, whatever the precise relation may be between Protestantism and the rise of capitalism—and probably the one thing which can safely be said about it is that any simple account is likely to be misleading—there is manifestly some connection, and the fact of this connection is an example of the ambiguity which attaches to success. One hesitates to raise questions over matters where one has no competence, but was Marx doing justice to the situation where he saw the division of labor and the establishment of a distance between the laborer and his or her work as an example only of alienation? Is it not also a consequence of the employment of scientific method, which abstracts, breaks things down to their component parts, and rearranges them to produce results which yield new meanings and new possibilities? Is not this highly creative, even if it may also sometimes cost more than it is worth because of its dehumanizing effect?

What is undeniable is that it has produced a great deal of new wealth and that, as our argument has led us to expect, this has also created new difficulties. Partly because of the ambiguous way in which the wealth has been created, it has not always been obvious to know what to do with it. Clearly, because the rewards of effort are most unevenly distributed, a great deal of redistribution needs to take place through taxation and other means, and Christian teaching about mutual dependence should strongly support such moves toward equality.[6] But this is still not enough, because there will be a surplus to spend, and communities will have such a surplus even when individuals do not.

If we are the liberated rich, we badly need a Christian doctrine of how to spend in modern terms. Protestants should be particularly good at this, but there is little evidence that they are. Those who believe in justification by faith should have a "spending" rather than that "accumulating" ethic which the "Protestant ethic" is alleged to be, because accumulation leads to work-righteousness, the building up of a treasury of merit. Just as the primary impulse for action in the world for those justified by faith stems from gratitude for what God has done, so the main emphasis of Christians in dealing with the goods and possessions they have, material and spiritual, is on giving, and in doing so with generosity and imagination. So far, little thought has been given to what this should involve. The way taken by most rich Protestant individuals and families has been through the establishment of foundations, where giving becomes a professional exercise. This is a remarkable feature of American life and, when all allowance is made for the tax advantage it may sometimes bring, its beneficiaries should have the magnanimity to acknowledge its generosity and sense of responsibility. Yet, from a Christian point of view, this is only a partial solution because it represents what might be called the clericalism of giving. When offices in the church are overconcentrated in the hands of a professional clergy, it may be a sign of a desire to do things well, but it is also an indication of declining vitality on the part of those who are only too happy to hand over functions to the clergy. Similarly, to hand over the disposal of wealth to foundations is a sign that it is regarded as a serious matter which needs care and attention, but also that those who create or inherit the wealth lack the time or the insight to know how to spend it.

In saying this, the last thing I should want to suggest is that we should waste our substance in riotous living, but work creates wealth and wealth, in its turn, creates problems. To know how to spend wealth is at least as much a matter of Christian responsibility as to work hard and to be prepared to make sacrifices. Nor can the problem be solved by giving all our possessions away. It is true that this is what the rich young ruler was told to do, and this is what some may still have to do. It may even be that our whole civilization will not be saved until it learns again what material and spiritual poverty mean.[7] But even to sell all and give to the poor is not a simple operation, and in the complex modern world it could be peculiarly difficult. One has to consider the effect of the disposal of great possessions on their recipients, let alone on the balance of payments. This is even more true of spiritual possessions than of material ones, and it is true enough of the latter. We might be doing no more than wishing our problems on to others, saying to them in effect, "Here, take them and see whether you can do better," and we might find the recipients increasingly reluctant to accept them. That has been an element, although in fairness no more than one element, in the attitude with which Britain has divested itself of the inherited colonial reponsibilities, and it is not entirely admirable.

On the basis of what has already been said about the nature of maturity, it is possible to see some of the ways in which the creative power of work should express itself so that it promotes rather than hinders our own entry to the kingdom, and in doing so promotes that of others also.

First, the more successful our work is and the richer we become as a result, the more important it is to improve the work's quality and to be discriminating about what we do. Most new things have to be bought at a price, and we should become increasingly sensitive to the question of whether the price we have to pay for our prosperity is worth paying, especially when we remember that some of the heaviest bills take a long time to come in. This has become increasingly clear in these days in relation to our material environment when the degree of pollution and ultimate poverty which the pursuit of short-term prosperity involves has become inescapably obvious, but more is involved in it from a Christian point of view than is usually considered. In discussing the church's institutional prosperity, we shall see how vital it is that it should strike deeper roots as it grows if it is not to wither and die in the next generation. This works even more rapidly in the ordinary life of society, especially modern highly industrialized society, because it is always disposed, unless it meets stern resistance, to produce not what is most necessary for the community's health but what can be most readily and profitably made and sold in the largest possible market, and this means standardization and increasing triviality.

This is why the richer we become, the more we need to educate ourselves for maturity, to be stimulated into new kinds of creative action, and to be taught both how to give and how to be more discriminating over what we ourselves consume. Once again, this is as important in relation to the things of the mind and spirit as it is to material goods. Many of the good things of this life are too readily available in these spheres also in the Western world. They are poured out endlessly through modern media of communication, including formal education itself. It has all become more than most of us can take in. The response becomes pitifully superficial because we have not been able properly to "mark, learn, and inwardly digest" one great experience before another crowds in upon us. All this rich diet is proving too much for us, especially as we already show signs of becoming fat and slothful. The only way out, as we have seen, is harder and better work. When we really try to meet our great responsibilities in the modern world, then we shall need and be able to burn up all the energy provided by the good things which are so readily available.

Second, work breeds wealth and, in the long term if not always in the short, the better the work the greater the wealth. But wealth stimulates covetousness. The more we have, the more we want. This is partly because it becomes progressively more difficult and more expensive to maintain the same level of satisfaction as that which was originally received from the enjoyment of prosperity,[8] and partly because we come more and more to put our trust in our possessions. We both want them to grow and to be secure, to put them out to usury and, at the same time, to place them where neither moth nor rust (inflation) can erode nor thieves (the government) break through and steal. The two aims are incompatible, so we become anxious and deserve our Lord's rebuke. The best cure for this anxiety is better and more useful work, undertaken according to an order of priorities different from that which the pursuit of wealth alone imposes. Experience amply confirms this. When one is absorbed in doing worthwhile work which calls out one's best capacities, anxiety evaporates. Just as great responsibility evokes humility, so worthwhile work demands the concentration which leaves no room for worry. Similarly, those who find real satisfaction in their work have no more than a marginal interest in the extraneous rewards it brings, such as the size of the paycheck which is such an endless cause of squalid dispute in these days. They literally have better things to think about. This is true of work in general. It should be supremely true of the work of those who have a vocation to seek first God's kingdom and his righteousness.

This attitude should not only mean release from the curse of covetousness but should also enable us to be generous and joyful. This, in its turn, should affect the way in which wealth is shared and work found and apportioned. Mature Christian civilization should be able to pass on to other societies the benefits, material and spiritual, which wealth has brought it, along with the resources necessary for their proper use while, at the same time, helping those who receive them to learn from its mistakes. The poorer peoples of the world are obviously not well served when they are encouraged to move from the frugal simplicity of a pastoral existence and uproot themselves from their families and the social contact to which they are accustomed in order to engage in repetitive work in mines or factories and to spend much of their extra money income on baubles which provide dubious satisfactions. The present surge of interest in so-called intermediate technology is a belated recognition of the truth of this. It must not be allowed to have only the short life of a fashionable novelty. It has arisen out of genuine Western self- criticism,[9] and its implementation will demand skill and persistence and the readiness to fight powerful vested interests in the poorer nations themselves just as much as in the richer.

It was the Protestant countries which, for good or for ill, took the initiative in starting the Industrial Revolution. It would be wonderful if they had the will to take a similarly energetic initiative in repairing its damage. They have greater resources for doing so than either they or their critics often suppose. Partly because they are so self-critical, they are often the victims of their own caricatures. The actual ethics of the most characteristically Protestant of Protestant communities in modern times have not borne very much relation to the "Protestant ethic" of popular sociology. They may have suffered from complacency, but they have certainly not been joyless and penny-pinching. More nonsense has been written about the Puritans and their descendants than about any other social group. Even on the material level, it has been countries like Scotland, Holland, Canada, New Zealand, and parts of the USA and England which, over the years, have produced many of the finest goods and achieved the highest level of job satisfaction for the largest number of people. One of the greatest and least regarded achievements of the USA has been its combination of zest in work with joy in giving, which is very refreshing by comparison with the grumbling shabby-gentility of so much modern British life. This is not due simply to the youth of the nation, as disparaging critics allege, but is an achievement of maturity.

One of the reasons why American work and giving possess these qualities of zest and generosity is that they also have within them an element of play. This is the surest sign that they are the fruit of growing maturity rather than of inexperience. The more we succeed in redeeming work from the curse of Adam, the more like play it should become. "All work and no play makes Jack a dull boy." More than that, it is likely to make him a listless and inefficient workman, a worried workman who lacks sufficient detachment and imagination to enjoy what he is doing. Protestants, of all people, should know this because, if there is anything their basic insights should teach them, it is the dangers of work-righteousness, so that even the most worthwhile, socially useful work should not be taken all the time with complete seriousness. There should be no Protestant doctrine of work without a Protestant doctrine of play.

Once again, the extent to which traditional Protestant culture has failed to see this point has been grossly exaggerated by its critics.[10] It is not generally known that even John Calvin used to play bowls with John Knox and other friends in Geneva on Sunday evenings, and insufficient attention has certainly been paid to the fact that most of the great team games of the modern world were invented and initially developed in Protestant communities.[11] But work-righteousness is so pervasive that it creeps into our play, as any American football coach or British soccer manager can testify, so that even our play needs to be redeemed if it is itself not to share in the curse of Adam.

As far as the inner life of the church is concerned, the place to begin this redemption is with the institution of the Lord's day. The Lord's day is not only the festival of the resurrection but also the day which incorporates, in a Christian context, the insights of the Jewish Sabbath. As Barth has observed, it is appropriate that what was the Sabbath day according to the Genesis story for the Creator should be the first of days for the Lord's creatures. It is the day on which we are to stand back from our everyday occasions and look at them in the perspective of eternity, taking heart from the knowledge that God's kingdom is our home and rejoicing in the way in which things are moving toward the fulfillment of God's original intention in creation.

The element of play should be present in this sense, that on this day we pretend briefly that we are already redeemed, so that we can return refreshed to face the mundane realities of life on this earth during the rest of the week. The pretense does not lie in supposing that the heavenly country exists when it does not, but in the playful assumption that we are already there while we are still on this earth. This is the real point of reducing all secular activity to a minimum, putting on our best clothes, and treating each other with special dignity. The meaning has been lost when this is regarded as an expression of legalism, of "strictness." It is meant to be a celebration, a discipline of fulfillment and happiness. We look at each other briefly as though we were already glorified. The Christian vision of the world to come is no impoverished retreat from reality. It is an imaginative apprehension of a life fuller than our present capacities are able to express, so that there has to be an element of pretense, of play, in our attempts to anticipate that life. Yet, as with the play of children, the effort involved in acting the role of being more grown-up than we really are, indirectly trains us for greater maturity and strengthens us for meeting the more intractable challenges of every day.

The decline of the full enjoyment of the Lord's day has undoubtedly diminished us in our ability both to work and to play aright. It is a sign that horizons have shrunk when instead of looking at their lives in the perspective of eternity, so many people are content to fill up their Sundays simply with journalistic interpretations of the week's events. Christians do sometimes succumb to a false otherworldliness, but that is hardly a serious threat at present. The world to come is not only what lies beyond the grave, it is also the world of the future into which Israel believed that their God was calling them and where the divine name and nature would be made known only as the people were called into a new situation. This is the basic stimulus to new creation which, in this sense, always has to be otherworldly. It gives urgency and courage to the effort to bring something new into being and the ability to persevere when the originality of what is being created prevents others from recognizing its value.[12]

The Lord's day will not recover its refreshing quality by being made more relaxing nor yet, as some liturgical experiments which rightly seek to reemphasize its elements of celebration try to do, by following the world's fashion of what is supposed to be lively and spontaneous.

It has to provide renewal for those who are hungry and thirsty after their struggles in the world and, while it is true that their jaded appetites may need a little judicious stimulation, what they require most is solid sustenance, which builds them up into maturity and gives them strength for the next stages of their journey.

This does not require that the element of play should be over-looked, even in worship. The Lord's day is the main working day for professional ministers, and they should conduct themselves with the diligence and competence of professionals, but should also not forget that they are leaders of a celebration, in the preaching as well as at the Lord's table. Ministers sometimes give the impression on the Lord's day of being more consumed with worldly anxiety than any tycoon determined to keep ahead in the rat race, rushing to do too many things according to the tightest of schedules, trying like Martha to justify themselves by being cumbered about with much serving. It is on the Lord's day above all else that the Lord's people should be those of gentle spirit, peacemakers, magnanimous, generous, and joyful. The servants of the church's service can help them become this by keeping the tension and strain involved in their own service firmly in the background and by striving to make public worship express the order and composure, and occasionally the silence, of the world to come.

Their celebration of the Lord's day should be normative for the way in which they enjoy recreation, but play has a place on other levels of experience as well, for even the most mature of Christians. It also has a negative justification, as a way of coping with some of the inescapable limitations of our fallen nature. None of us is yet fully redeemed, nor are we likely to be while we remain on this earth. We all suffer from what might be described as the hangover of evolution, possessing deeply rooted within ourselves aggressive, combative, and competitive urges, which often make us anything but gentle in spirit, makers of peace, and magnanimous, even when we set out with the best intentions to be so. If we pretend that we are entirely free of these urges, we are probably being guilty of humbug; or if they are so weak in us as to be safely ignored, then either we are remarkably far advanced on the road to sanctity or, more probably, we are lacking in that natural vitality which is regarded as normally and even admirably human. These qualities are very visible in children, and we know that controlled play is a civilized way of channeling and releasing these energies in a harmless, enjoyable , and sometimes a socially constructive way. Adults also need games in which it is right to want to win and to be disappointed if you lose, to be shamelessly and cheerfully partisan, and even to show off a little. It is essential, however, that we keep within the rules and that the games be treated as forms of play and not as part of the serious business of living. It is good to play hard, but it is essential to play fair and to keep one's sense of proportion. For this reason, Christian maturity has an interest, which our allegedly oversolemn predecessors saw more clearly than we do, in preventing games from becoming too professionalized and linked with politics, national prestige, and religion, altogether more serious than work and certainly than vocation. We may again have to enter arenas that used to be centers of recreation but have increasingly become more like places of gladiatorial combat to try to bring back play to sport. Things have reached such a pitch that probably some of us will have to be thrown to the lions in order to do so.[13]

But the positive side of the justification of play is the more important. It may be necessary sometimes to relax from the strains which vocation imposes and to behave like children, but it should be more characteristic of the followers of Christ to celebrate the strength of their maturity. This is done chiefly through their grateful service to their neighbors, and through the superabundance of that service, but it should also be done through their ability to enjoy themselves, to share enjoyment with each other, and to spread enjoyment around. "See how these Christians love one another," the surprised ancient world said and was impressed. The modern world would be even more surprised and impressed if it were compelled to say, "See how these Christians enjoy one another." We have become so conscious of strain today that the notion of having a surplus of energy may seem unreal, yet mature Christians should occasionally find themselves in situations where they have time and energy to do things for no other reason than to express their joy in living. Only when this kind of mastery is achieved, when in Augustine's phrase we use the world to enjoy God and through God are able to enjoy the world, do we come near maturity and can be trusted with success.

12

A Mature Church

ONE OF THE most tantalizingly elusive sections of Bonhoeffer's *Letters and Papers from Prison*[1] is that in which he speaks of a world come of age and of the difference which this demands in the attitudes of Christian spokesmen. I have taken part in many discussions of what he might have meant, where good arguments have been put forward on behalf of various, and possibly contradictory, interpretations, and have reached the conclusion that, beyond a point, speculation becomes unprofitable. After all, he was not writing a doctoral thesis but throwing out a fresh idea in a letter written from prison to a friend. While I am confident, therefore, that the first point I wish to make is very much in the spirit of what Bonhoeffer was beginning to express in his *Letters and Papers,* it would be too much to claim his authority for it. The notion of a world come of age demands that we also think of the church as a community of those who have come of age. No Christian believer, least of all one with Bonhoeffer's convictions,[2] can accept the idea that the world reaches any positive maturity without reference to its Creator, as though it possessed an independent vitality of its own that enables human reason progressively to liberate itself into some kind of abstract apprehension of pure truth, uncorrupted by all the errors of the past. This is the possibility which has captivated reflective Europeans ever since Descartes shut himself up in his room beside his stove and resolved to doubt the existence of everything except God and himself as a thinking subject. God gradually dissolved into nonentity as a result of this process, and finally Sartre and others discovered that the thinking subject itself also dissolved, leaving only intolerable contingency with which no one can live. If there is any positive sense in which the world has come of age, it must be because it has been *given* maturity, which means freedom, choice, accountability, and limitation in relationship and in cohumanity. That is to say, it has been given maturity of the same kind as that which is claimed for those who know God in Christ.

The Christian claim is that there is only one kind of maturity, only one form of true humanity, whose nature has been made clear in Jesus Christ.[3] It may have adumbrations and developments in areas of experience which bear no direct relation to the community of Christian experience. What these are and how they are related to Christ is the subject of constant debate within the Christian community itself, but the Christian claim loses its point if what is revealed concerning humankind's nature and destiny in Jesus Christ is not normative for the understanding of humanity as a whole. The fact of Christ means that the race has not developed by accident but in the providence of God. Christian anthropology stands or falls by the claim that it is true anthropology. This is the theme worked out with such confident amplitude in Barth's *Church Dogmatics* III and IV. The church is intended to be the community which consciously organizes its life on the basis of the belief that, whether it likes it or not, humankind has come of age because, in the fullness of time, God sent his Son. This holds for all humankind, but it is the church's responsibility to witness to the universality of this truth by the way in which it expresses the recognition of it within its own life.

If this is so, nothing could be more beside the point than to suppose, as some current Christian discussion seems to, that the world has one kind of maturity and the church another, and that the church, therefore, has "problems" about how to address a world come of age. There may, of course, be circumstances in which those outside the church may be speaking more truly mature words than those within,[4] but there are no "problems" about these which cannot be solved by more genuine obedience on the church's part. Insofar as they are words of maturity, they make a bond between those within and outside the church, and communication between them becomes that much easier. What the church has to say to the world is essentially the same as what it has to say to itself, although it may find it expedient to use different language in the one case from the other. Our destiny is now clear. Through Christ, we have become the children of God, who have the inescapable burdens and privileges of their freedom. We are grown up. It is time we started to act our age and stopped behaving like infants or adolescents. We must take the sustenance which God provides for adults, meat not milk, and build each other up, so that we can rise to the height of our calling.

This is not only congruous with the spirit of Bonhoeffer, in his insistence that to be Christian is to be fully human and that the church must be in the center of the village and not at its margin, but it is also in keeping with the basic insights of the Reformation, especially as expressed in Luther's primary tract on *The Freedom of the Christian Man*. Perhaps it is also worth saying in these days with reference to the doctrine of the church that it is very much in harmony with the authentic spirit of the ecumenical movement, certainly as its leaders at the time of the formation of the World Council of Churches at Amsterdam in 1948 understood it. Their emphasis on the worldwide mission of the whole Christian community and their reaction against narrow clericalism and self-centered denominationalism were an attempt to make the church see that, as the Amsterdam Assembly preparatory papers tried to show,[5] its task is to accept the responsibilities of maturity as humanity come of age.

I hope it will be sufficiently clear by now that this attitude is poles apart from ecclesiastical triumphalism and different also from that Christian neocolonialism with which the ecumenical movement is sometimes charged. It is true that the church is committed to try to make life on this earth a colony of heaven and that this must arouse the resistance of those whose loyalties lie elsewhere, but the church's safeguard against making this merely another form of human arrogance is that its first and chief enemies are those of its own household, not those who claim openly to serve other gods. The church cannot offer a share in its maturity to those outside or presume to build on any maturity it already finds in the world until it has begun to act its own age. And this the church cannot do until it takes into account all that has been said about power and the perils of riches.

The dangers of triumphalism and of Christian imperialism, arising from pride, can never be discounted, but more characteristic of churches today are those which come from complacency and sloth. Barth speaks of dispiritedness as an advanced form of the sin of sloth, and it is that dispiritedness, together with the mean and shrunken imagination which goes with it, which afflicts Christendom today. This may be more true of Britain than America, especially since the ecumenical movement has lost much of its momentum, but there are wide reaches of American church life also, especially in older parts of the country, where this dispiritedness is present.

Any sociologist morbid enough to be interested in ecclesiastical pathology could easily divide churches according to the different ways in which they are guilty of settling contentedly for less than maturity. There are those who treat all, or nearly all, members of the church merely as ordinary human infants rather than those who enjoy the glorious liberty of the children of God. Either the laity are regarded as the dependent children of the clerical hierarchies who are called "Fathers" and who alone enjoy varying degrees of adult status, or else clergy and laity alike become merely childish, as happens in some forms of popular Protestantism, with the clergy fulfilling a role not unlike that of permissive primary school or kindergarten teachers. Or else, when a little more vitality is present, the church is regarded as a school of spiritual adolescence, whose members constantly exhort each other to be prophetic or even revolutionary, and who are at odds with the generation immediately before them while they eagerly reach out after responsibilities in which they lose interest once they are handed to them, all as ways of resolving their identity crisis.[6] This is a much healthier situation than the others, but a church growing toward maturity will be glad to pass through it as quickly as possible.

The most typical way in which churches deny their maturity is by behaving as though they have already retired. A contemptuous European once described America as a country which has passed from barbarism to decadence without going through the intervening stage of civilization. That is an observation so grotesquely unfair, except perhaps in relation to some aspects of the American communications industry, as to warrant no comment but an indignant snort, but it has to be admitted that a process not unlike that can be observed in the life of some churches in America and elsewhere. They may have started in a flush of evangelistic zeal but failed to develop an effective spiritual and intellectual tradition or to abound in the works of love. They may have tried to keep going for a time with doses of revivalist shock treatment but finally settled into stale routine, resisting all change and stirred only by nostalgia for an idealized past. Such churches are to be found mainly in Protestantism, but there are others, chiefly Roman Catholic or Orthodox, which seem to be able to maintain themselves in an attitude of more graceful retirement almost indefinitely.

The fact that so many churches have declined in this way means that the Christian community has a great deal still to do before most of its members can speak with any credibility to the world about acting with maturity. We ourselves have to see that the purpose of church order is not to consolidate existing institutions but to build up the people of God into maturity, and we have to be fully aware of how complicated an operation this is, which needs all the resources of the Spirit if it is to be achieved. This is the theme of the New Testament document most directly concerned with maturity, the letter to the Ephesians. Having celebrated Christ's victory over all the alien powers which try to make human life subservient to them, the writer prays that his readers may appropriate the rich heritage which is now theirs and know the power of God in whom the fullness of life dwells. The second chapter asks them to remember their former alienation and emphasizes the breaking down of all barriers in Christ, so that they can be built up into Christ in cohumanity. The third chapter carries on the theme of the richness of this inheritance, which is open to Gentiles as to Jews, and prays that they too may comprehend what is the breadth, length, and height and know the love of Christ which surpasses human knowledge. The fourth appeals to them to live up to this high calling and moves on to the classic passage in which it is explained how all the gifts of the Spirit, made available through the ascended Christ, are intended to promote their growth into maturity, which they find together in Christ. The rest of the letter is taken up with reminders of some of the ethical consequences of this and concludes with the appeal to put on the whole armor of God.

From the point of view of growth in the common life of the church, perhaps the key word is that of building up or edification. Two particular aspects of it need bringing out in this context. The one is the generous nature of the provision made for it and the other is that all these gifts can only be properly appropriated when they are shared. Rich growth on good soil and cooperation in growth: these are the marks of a living church. We have all received an undeserved legacy and as we gather together for the share-out, we discover that the conditions are that we have to use it, multiply it, and do this in the only possible way, by cooperating with each other. To take one's own portion and go off to spend it in a far country on one's own is to waste it and to deny the purpose of the whole enterprise.

The way of the world, mercifully tempered by natural affection and our common interest in self-preservation, is not to build each other up but to do each other down. It is precisely when we have a chance to build, and not merely to survive, that most of us are tempted to be egotistical, self-assertive, and competitive, envying each other's gifts and seeing them as threats rather than as reinforcements. So to deal with each other that we bring out the best in each other requires grace, which bears with it all those qualities which we have been considering. And it has to be genuine grace. If it is reduced to a technique, a way to win friends and influence people, it becomes exploitative, an indirect way of doing others down; or when it is not that, it is sentimental, covering up the realities of the situation and therefore not enabling us "to speak the truth" or "deal truly with one another," as it has been alternatively translated, in love and thus to grow into Christ.[7]

This is why Christian growth must always have maturity clearly in view as its goal. The encouragement, the building up, we give to each other has to be more than that of the nursery or of subadolescence. These are appropriate on some levels, for babes in Christ or, perhaps, for those so bruised and battered by the cruelty of the world or the misusings of religion that they need tender handling; but the needs of such people must not be the norm, as some forms of modern religious education and pastoral care make them out to be. If we are to help each other grow up, our attitude toward ourselves and each other must have a certain astringency. Our words to each other are to be with grace, but also seasoned with salt. One of the more unfortunate translations in modern ears of the word *parakletos* in the fourth Gospel is the "comforter." There is indeed legitimate Christian comfort, but it comes after, not before, struggle. It only comes at times when it is comfort rather than stimulus that we really need. The word "comforter" used to be used in Britain for the pacifier put into a baby's mouth for it to suck, and it was thought to be both unhygienic and to hinder weaning. In the nineteenth century, the flannel band wrapped around a child's middle to protect it against the winter's blasts was also called a "comforter." Many people regard religion as no more than the provision of a comforter in these senses. The better translation of *parakletos,* of course, is the "fortifier" or "bracer," the one who pulls us together and makes us face life as it is. There is an old Oxford story of Dr. Phelps, a Victorian provost of Oriel College, who maintained the ancient English practice of self-torture, now greatly neglected under decadent American influence, of taking a cold bath every morning, regardless of the weather. One raw winter's morning an undergraduate passing the open window of an unheated bathroom overheard a stern voice addressing its owner, "Be a man, Phelps, be a man," followed by a splash and a gasp. That is the kind of spirit in which believers should frequently encourage themselves and each other, if they are to be built up into maturity.

The nature of the church's basic ordinances makes it clear that this is the intention of the distinctive structure which the Christian community is meant to have in the world. Baptism, standing at the very door of that community, should have more of the nature of Dr. Phelps's experience than it has come to have in most churches. Without at this stage going into the vexing question of whether baptism should always be by immersion and the related question of whether it is right to baptize infants—and much can be said on both sides of these familiar issues—it cannot be denied that baptism by immersion, especially in cold northern climates, does have the advantage of underlining dramatically the only terms upon which new life in Christ is possible. It involves taking the plunge, a shock to the system, and it is natural that we should tremble on the brink.[8] This element must be retained in the structure of the life of the Christian community if growth into maturity is not to be misconceived as a natural flowering, with no awareness of radical discontinuity. If the baptism of the infant children of believers is to be justified, it can only be on the grounds that this awareness of discontinuity is so important that it must be a factor in the upbringing of the child in the Christian community from the very outset.

The Lord's Supper must be understood in the light of the same insight. The grace given in baptism must constantly be renewed if we are to be maintained in our new life. It is a life of struggle, and we are in persistent danger of falling away while, as we have seen, our very successes bring their own special temptations. This is why we need to be recalled sharply to the reality of our Lord's death and to the need to continue to show it forth until he comes. This does not diminish the Lord's Supper as a eucharistic occasion, as a celebration, but it is necessary as a reminder of the only terms on which we can participate in our Lord's victory without being corrupted by what it brings us. Likewise, its emphasis on the corporate character of our life in Christ is a reminder in the same breath that, as Paul had to tell the Corinthians on the very occasion when he recalled the words of institution, our gathering together may itself become a way of doing each other down rather than of building each other up unless we discern the Lord's body in the midst, forgive each other, and establish our relations with each other afresh as members of his body.

It is from this point of view also that the proclamation of the word must be considered. If more is said about this, it is not because it is necessarily more significant than baptism and the Lord's Supper—in these days when Christian spokesmen can so easily say the wrong things, these actions may be more effective forms of proclamation— but because it provides the most readily articulated example, in Protestant churches especially, of the way in which the ordinances of the church are meant to be directed toward building up.

At the outset, it must be made clear that church proclamation is much more than a matter of sermons delivered by professional ministers. The Reformed tradition has undoubtedly suffered because, in practice, it has tended to identify the two.[9] Christ is known only in cohumanity. It is the whole body of the church, therefore, which proclaims Christ. We have to proclaim Christ to each other, in the mutual dependence of the body where each part counts,[10] and to do so together in our relationship with the world. It is a travesty of what is meant to happen to suppose that the word is delivered to the professional maker of sermons on the Sinai of his or her study on Saturday mornings, with the telephone off the hook so that no one can interrupt the minister's hot line to the Almighty, and then passed on to the waiting people on Sunday morning, when they take a brief holiday from their customary worship of the golden calf. For any minister to imagine such a thing is either to fall into an egotistical complacency which disqualifies him or her from hearing the word or else, if the minister is more aware of what is involved, it is to try to carry a burden of responsibility greater than any individual can bear, precisely the burden which has been removed from our shoulders by our Lord in his declaration of the word.

It is Christ who speaks the word, and he does so in the Spirit through the testimony of prophets and apostles as the Scriptures record it and through what his people come to know of him in his dealings with them throughout the ages. For the hearing and the continued proclamation of the word, his people receive gifts and these gifts are varied in character. "Some are gifted to be apostles, some prophets, some evangelists, some pastors and teachers to equip God's people for work in his service, to the building up of the body of Christ."[11] It is true that, whether rightly or wrongly, the exercise of many of these gifts, although not all of them, has been concentrated in Protestant churches in the conventional action of the delivery of sermons in the course of public worship. These exercises have often, although by no means invariably, proved themselves throughout the ages to be truly edifying. But the fact remains that, in themselves, they are not the primary form of the proclamation of the word of God in Christ by the church. They are a help, designed to enable the church to hear and obey more effectively what he is saying to the whole community. It is a service, to be hoped always a spiritually gifted service, of the church's service of God. In the sermon, as elsewhere in worship, minister and people wait together upon their Lord. The minister's privilege and responsibility, great enough for any mortal being, is so to lead his or her Christian colleagues that together they can hear the word with the maximum of clarity and the minimum of distortion. All gifts will be needed for this, but ministers will also be dependent on the gifts of the congregation, not least if they are to be helped to get themselves out of the way, so that their action is truly one of service and not secretly one of exploitation. To hark back to the analogy with Sinai, the model in this context for the minister is not Moses but Aaron. Moses is the archetype of the apostolic community as a whole, Aaron of its mouthpiece, the minister.[12]

All this should not be taken simply as yet another plea for fewer sermons or for more experiments with other forms of communication within the church. Such experiments may be desirable, although enthusiasts for them do well to remember that, in a time of confusion like the present, they are extremely difficult and the failure rate is likely to be high. We are on safer ground if we begin, at least, by taking more time and trouble to do better what we have been long trained to do and what people have some experience of knowing how to receive from us. That there should be far more interchange between ministers and people about the interpretation of Scripture than usually exists today, with far more corporate Bible study and systematic group theological study, is manifest. That hardly comes under the heading of experiment, since there used to be more of it in the past than there is now. In a church growing toward maturity, there should be an increasing diversity of gifts and a growing competence and freedom in self-expression among the members. Experience shows that this will make more and not less demands on the services of the professional preachers of sermons by raising more pertinent questions in the life of the congregation and a more alert and expectant attitude in trying to listen for the answers. This may or may not mean the production of more sermons than we have today. It will certainly mean better ones.

This is an important matter because, even when the sermon is cut down to its proper size, it remains one of the chief ways in which the members of the church, when they gather together, can encourage each other and build each other up. This, above all, is a place where, echoing Bonhoeffer's phrase, we speak to each other in strength and discover what is "wisdom among the mature,"[13] and we badly need to recover the pulpit's proper function. For all the present talk of the decline of preaching and about the need for other forms of communication, there must be as many sermons delivered in churches today as there were in the Victorian heyday of popular preaching, even though they are certainly very much shorter. Today less trouble is taken over their preparation, both minister and congregation are more confused about their true function, and sermons have become far less significant events. The result is that the growth of the whole church toward maturity is gravely hampered.

What preachers have to avoid should be obvious enough. They should not talk down to people, nor "chat them up," a procedure normally associated with attempted seduction. Above all, they should not trivialize the material committed to their charge. If they are to help people hear the word, they have to do their part in enlarging the understanding and the imagination of their hearers, and this means effort and strain on both sides. They must totally reject what still passes for the sermon in too many congregations, the serving of rehashed everyday trivia about the surface of events, washed up on polluted metropolitan shores and salvaged by beachcombing journalists. Their professional responsibility is to help people hear and understand the Bible, and with it the best wisdom of the Christian past, and this requires a competence, thoroughness, and accountability to their peers at least equal to that with which other members of the great professions discharge their responsibilities. But it must also exemplify the qualities of maturity, together with the most acute sensitivity to its dangers. No one who has tried it will pretend that this is easy. Great efforts of translation and interpretation are necessary before people can be helped to hear the veritable word of God on levels sufficiently deep to nourish real growth. The trouble with a great deal of modern preaching is that it has concluded that the task is impossible before it has been tried, or tried with a degree of effort remotely commensurate with the magnitude of the task. It has fallen into Barth's sin of "dispiritedness," an advanced form of the sin of sloth.

Two actions within the competence of churches as they exist today are necessary if the pulpit is to recover its proper function in ministering to growth toward maturity. The first is the reestablishment of rigorous professional standards in relation to the theological task, which must be undertaken if sermons worthy of the name are to be produced again. It may be valuable also to learn the arts of successful communication in the modern mode, but that is, at best, a supplement to and no kind of substitute for the preacher's distinctive task. It remains as true as it ever was that if we take care of the sense, the sound will, in the end, take care of itself. It is a corruption of the Reformed understanding of the church when the professional ministry is thought of as the source of all the gifts which should inhere in the Christian community—those of counseling, administration, initiative, education, healing, social service, prophetic leadership. All are valuable and some may need so to be structured as to have their own professionalism. It is to be expected that ministers of the word will possess one or more of these gifts as well as those which belong to their own function, but it must not be assumed that they should possess all of them. They are not spiritual "leaders,"[14] which is a dubious secular conception. When the expectation is that they should be, the good Lord tends to confound the church by denying it the gifts of ministry, leaving it only with a kind of failed leader, the pathetic figure which too many ministers appear to have become. The ministers' specialty is the service of the word and, if they exercise it diligently, as "workmen not ashamed," they will again compel attention by the way in which they bring out the quality of the material they have to handle.

This will do more than anything else to help bring about the other condition which must be fulfilled if the pulpit is to function properly again. The other members of the church must regain a right understanding of their own function within the church. When there was a sharp decline in the number of candidates coming forward for ministerial training in the USA several years ago, a church "organization man" explained it as due to the renewed emphasis on the vocation of the laity, which was such a feature of the ecumenical movement in the forties and fifties. People were beginning to conclude, he said, that they could be good Christians without having to become professional ministers. If that were really the case, which I do not believe for a moment, the churches of the present time have been saved from having to carry the burden of a large number of bad ministers. Once again, the greatest stimulus a professional minister can obtain for doing his or her own job properly is to find other Christians doing theirs, thus developing an appetite for the food he or she exists to help serve to them.

This is why a church growing into maturity will be careful so to organize itself that other members as well as professional ministers will have opportunity to "deal truly with each other in love," which will include taking initiatives in relation to interpretation of the word as well as commenting on interpretations offered by the minister. This is particularly true of those who carry heavy responsibilities in the general life of humankind and who may be given insights denied to the professional minister unless he or she is prepared seriously to listen to them as their servant. Perhaps the gravest weakness of a clericalist conception of ministerial office is that it prevents this from happening and thus impoverishes the church's understanding of what God is saying to all people.[15] I do not much like the phrase "lay theologians," but a church growing toward maturity will possess many members of that type.[16] It was a sign of genuine revival when, largely under the influence of the ecumenical movement, so many of them emerged in the immediate postwar period, as it is a sign of decline that their numbers now appear to have diminished. Some progress has been made in the meantime to fill up the missing half of the church's life. The pews are not as comfortable, nor their occupants as somnolent, as they were, but the churches are still overclericalized. The "godly discipline" of the Reformed tradition, interpreted in the charitable, life-affirming spirit of the New Testament, remains extremely fragmentary even in those churches which are proudest of their Reformed heritage. In these days, they are often put to shame by the way in which the "apostolate of the laity" is fulfilled in the Roman Catholic Church. Until this situation alters, we shall continue to provide clearer examples of the consequences of complacency and sloth than of what mature humanity can be.

Even in this situation, however, churches are not without their riches, and therefore also the problems that riches bring. In particular, they possess the inheritance of the institutional remnants of past success. A clear understanding of what maturity means can do much to help them deal with these in ways which promote and do not frustrate their true purpose.

To illustrate, a living church usually grows, numerically, financially, and as an organization, as well as in terms of spiritual maturity. That is, it inevitably becomes an institution, occupying a "space" in the world, in Bonhoeffer's phrase, but for many practical purposes it is no different from the spaces occupied by other institutions. It undertakes other functions than the maintenance and the reflection upon the means of grace. It becomes an employer of labor, an educational establishment, a social service organization, a caterer, and much else beside. It is not always appreciated, even by church people, what a great deal of space churches do occupy in the world. The Roman Catholic Church is reputed to be the largest single employer of labor, apart from some state military and civil establishments, in the whole world. This is inevitable, and can be done with grace, but a church has to see that its very success along these lines will interfere with growth toward maturity unless these two considerations are kept in mind.

First, the church will be at pains to distinguish clearly between its various institutional functions and will have very firm priorities. Of all bodies, the church should know that the more good things are added unto it, the more its earthly kingdom expands, the easier it becomes to lose sight of the fact that it is meant first to seek God's kingdom and his righteousness. Apart from anything else, if the church fails to make these distinctions, it will use on one level attitudes and procedures which are appropriate only on another. That is the road to the sanctimonious incompetence which disfigures some church organizations. Thus, it is right for the church to ask members to make sacrifices for the sake of the kingdom, "to give and not to count the cost; to fight and not to heed the wounds; to toil and not to seek for rest; to labor and not to ask for any reward" but, in doing so, the church must be quite sure that it is for the sake of the kingdom that it is asking them, and not for some everyday purpose of the church as one earthly organization among others. The relation between the kingdom and the church is never one of identity and it is only the Lord, and never any church official *ex officio,* however personally dedicated he or she may be, who has the right to ask for that kind of sacrifice because only the Lord can lead us to the level of experience where strength can be found genuinely and acceptably to make it. To use the fact that a call to such sacrifice is always a possibility, and that we must keep in training to be ready for it, as an excuse for tightfistedness or sharp practice in the ordinary relationships of life is to be guilty of the sin of Simon Magus (Acts 8), generally in these days without being able even to offer the slight compensation of a share in the excitement of his false charisma.

Likewise, as one organization among others in the world, the church should nevertheless behave as a community of the rich, but one which has been made to realize the perils of riches. What is distinctive about the church's attitude is that it should do this regardless of whether, by the standards of the world, it happens to be materially well off or not. Take an example from what is sometimes thought of as one of the most delicate matters of all, that of the payment received by those concerned most directly with the service of the sanctuary, professional ministers. In Britain since the Second World War—the situation is significantly different in the USA where the churches have enjoyed more recent institutional prosperity— churches have had relatively little money with which to pay ministers and, let it be said, even less with which to pay other servants of the sanctuary like church musicians. In itself, this need not matter very much. Those who perform these services are not in it for the money and, in the things which matter most, they are rich people, but the attitude which a church adopts in such a situation matters a great deal. Suppose a church were to say to a minister, or to any other paid church officer: "You know the situation as well as we do. We cannot pay you as much as we should like and we know, of course, that it is not comparable to what you could probably obtain doing other work, but it is the best that we can do. As soon as things improve, we shall not need any prompting from you to see that you share fully in our good fortune, and any suggestion you have about making things easier we shall most sympathetically consider. The important thing is that we all do our best to ensure that you are set free as much as possible for your essential task, which cannot be computed in monetary terms." In a situation like that, most ministers can accept low pay cheerfully and the attitude of their congregation helps to build them up, to make them appreciate how rich they really are.[17] But if a church gets into the frame of mind where it feels self-righteous about the poverty of its paid servants and assumes that it need not be unduly concerned about it because the going rate in this particular market has usually been low, this inevitably breeds resentment which drags down and impoverishes both ministers and people. The trouble lies not in unavoidable material poverty but in a thoughtless misuse of the riches of dedication and loyalty on which the church can call. Like all rich people, churches like to have large numbers of domestic servants, and they should be sufficiently gracious and aware of the temptations of riches to know how to treat them aright. The church's inner life must express the considerate, harmonious, generous, magnanimous, and joyful nature of the gospel by which it claims to live.

The other consideration is no less fundamental. The church exists to proclaim the good news of where true humanity is to be found and to exemplify in the midst of this present world what growth toward maturity in Christ means. Thus the Spirit calls people out of the world and gathers them into church order, which is much more than institutional organization since it is meant to reflect the order of the coming kingdom rather than that of this world which is passing away. For this purpose, they need to assemble frequently to spend much time together, to offer praise and prayer, to encourage and build each other up, and to wait upon the Lord in his word that they may consider reordering their lives in the light of his will as they strive to move toward the fullness of their life in Christ. All this most Christians recognize. It is not so widely recognized that, having gathered, they must also scatter. Their lives are not meant to be lived only in the fellowship of believers. That would make them again to be a saved remnant out of the world rather than a saving remnant in the world. They have to move out into the world, both in order to bring others to the knowledge of the truth and to express their vows of obedience in their daily lives, striving to transform the common life of this passing world into the image of the coming kingdom. A church which tries to grow toward maturity will see that its growth depends as much on effective scattering as upon gathering, and it will never allow the one to suffer at the expense of the other.

While the professional ministry must inevitably be preoccupied with what happens to the church when it gathers, it has an equal responsibility to help ensure that, having gathered, it also scatters. One of its modest achievements in several Western lands in the years immediately after the Second World War was that some of its members took the initiative in encouraging the revival of Christian vocation in the world which took place at that time, expressed by the many activities promoted by or associated with the World Council of Churches. This did not happen quite as much in the USA as it did in Europe, partly perhaps because the need for it was not so glaringly obvious, and it may be important for American church people to bear this in mind in planning their strategy for the future. The last thing I should want to do is to disparage the great church-building boom which the USA experienced in the period up to the early 1960s, which has already suffered from being undervalued rather than otherwise. The opportunity for horizontal expansion was there, and it was right to thrust in that particular sickle with all the vigor that the lively American churches possess. The amount of devotion and sheer hard work which went into the enterprise deserves the respectful admiration of the rest of the world's Christian community. Yet the temptation obviously existed to regard ecclesiastical empire building as equivalent to the extension of the kingdom and thus to create an ever larger buffer state between the kingdom and the world, having its own laws, customs, and internal taxation system. When, as always happens with such booms, the period of expansion ends and the problems of maintaining this overextended empire in the style to which it has become accustomed multiply, the danger then is that those who have a vested interest in keeping it going, who are chiefly those professionally employed within it, will spend all their energies in dealing with its internal problems and become increasingly reluctant to encourage its members to scatter.

American resilience and self-criticism, along with continuing national expansion, may prove sufficient to enable its churches to avoid some of the mistakes which the British churches committed in the aftermath of their Victorian boom, but only if they see where the dangers lie. In their proper desire for greater unity, and the redeployment of resources which it ought to bring, church administrators should seek to prevent the creation of excessively large and complex new church structures, which take too many people and too much time and money to maintain and which, therefore, inevitably increase the size of the ecclesiastical buffer state at the very time when it should be contracting. On the other hand, the line taken recently by some "activist" young ministers in Britain and America is no less misleading. They conclude that they themselves should do the scattering and devote their energies to social work, general education, or political activity, calling these good works expressions of their distinctive ministerial functions. This is a misuse of their calling and implies a covert clericalism which would be as damaging to the integrity and maturity of the church as the overt clericalism of earlier times, if it had any hope of being anything as effective. The professional minister can best serve the church's service in the world by so interpreting the faith for people in church that they are eager to clear off church premises to get on with their real job, once the worship, study, discussion, and enjoyment of each other's company and the care for each other which should follow it are over. The presence of church mice finding room to make their nests on church premises is a sign of bad housekeeping. One very practical way in which ministers can help them clear off is by keeping church councils and committees and their agendas to the barest minimum and by setting an example to such activities in the outside world by the economy and dispatch with which the church's internal business is dealt with. Quaker meetings may not be a fully adequate form of public worship but other churches can learn things from them about the way in which their business should be conducted, not least the value of silence when nothing significant requires to be said and the promptness with which the meeting closes once the hour is struck. A mature Christian community should not need to spend much time in dealing with the details of its domestic affairs. These easily become a form of that "anxiety" rebuked in the Sermon on the Mount. There is much more urgent work to be done out there in the world. But it is to be done by those who have the responsibility and calling to do it, and it is officious for professional ministers to try to take that work from them, while still wishing to be regarded as professional ministers.

This is not to say, of course, that ministers of the word should not stand alongside their fellow Christians in the world and do so outside church premises. In the complexity of modern life, the need for chaplaincy constantly grows. It is true also, as it always has been, that when there is an urgent need in the world which no one else can meet, the minister has as much responsibility as anyone else for meeting it. Bonhoeffer found himself driven to such a situation, and it could be argued that things might not have come to such a pass in Germany if many other Lutheran ministers had come to the same conclusion much earlier. But that is not the same as saying that such activity is a form of the specialized ministry of the word. This was something which had to be done and there was no one else to do it. Any Christian might find himself or herself in such a situation; to assume that it is a form of the ministry of the word because a professional minister knows no exemption from it is dangerously to confuse functions. It also sometimes leads ministers to claim privileges which are justified only for the fulfillment of their proper office in contexts where they have no right to them. Clerics who enter the political arena, for example, sometimes claim protection from "the heat of the kitchen" because they wear clerical collars and believe they should be spared the kind of personal criticism from opponents which ordinary politicians have to learn to put up with.

Maturity is concerned with freedom, choice, limitation, responsibility, and accountability. This means that it is the person in a particular situation, whether in church, in private life, or in the general life of society, who is answerable to God for the way in which he or she behaves. The minister is there to help, and the closer he or she can get to that person in doing so, without getting in the way, the better. The minister of the word cannot presume to make the decision for that person or to usurp his or her place. Ministers who truly understand what their function is in trying to promote growth toward Christian maturity will be more than content with their distinctive ministerial role. It will take all their time and talents to be reasonably competent Aarons without aspiring to be Moseses as well.

The Interrelation of Church and Society

A church growing toward maturity will also strive to have a mature attitude toward the wider society in which it has its own space. The way to begin doing so is by considering the church as an institution in the context of other institutions of society with which it is bound to be involved. That may seem obvious enough, but the fact is curiously neglected in most discussions of the relation between churches and society. A great deal of attention has been paid, of course, to what the attitude of churches should be to other institutions, and to what the attitude of these others should be to churches. However, it has generally been with a view to safeguarding the institutional freedom and sometimes the privileges of churches, or else to ensuring that their interests are adequately reflected in the arrangements made by other bodies over matters where churches conceive themselves to be very directly concerned, such as the education of children or laws dealing with family life and sexual morality. And there is a vast body of material produced from a Christian viewpoint about the state, the economic order, education, international affairs, race relations, and a whole range of matters of public discussion. Yet in all this, it has not been common for theologians, in particular, to see the church as one institution, or group of institutions, among others in the general life of the world, itself an important factor in the give and take of social relationships.[18]

One reason for this may be that many of the theologians most deeply concerned for the well-being of society have had more radical views about society than those most deeply concerned for the institutional well-being of the church. This has been especially true of those elaborately structured and centralized churches, like the Roman Catholic, which would be most likely to be involved as major institutions with other institutions. Theologians have felt embarrassed, therefore, about bringing the church as an institution into the discussion because its own practice often appears to contradict what they are advocating for society as a whole. It has only been quite recently, over a few quite specific issues such as investment policy as it affects race relations, and the status of women, that there has been a partial change of attitude. It is noteworthy that Reinhold Niebuhr rarely applied the insights of his *Moral Man and Immoral Society*[19] to the institutional life of churches even though, on the face of it, they had as much relevance there as anywhere else and would have given ample scope for the play of his highly developed sense of irony. This may be partly explicable in American terms because the USA does not have that organic view of the whole of society, including church life, which is particularly characteristic of the more traditionalist forms of English society and prefers, as the Constitution lays down, to emphasize the independence rather than the interdependence of society's major institutions. But this is not the only reason because this gap in thinking also exists in British and in more general ecumenical discussion.

Why should it matter that churches should be thought about in this way? Because it is a sign that they are approaching their task in the world with the concreteness which the New Testament requires. In his analysis of the Pauline notion of the church as the body of Christ, Ernst Käsemann[20] has brought out how very specifically, almost literally, this metaphor was meant. If we take the much abused term "secuiarization," as I prefer to do, in a neutral, descriptive sense to mean the church's attempt to express in terms of the conditions of life today insights which derive from a reality which comes from beyond this world, we can regard the church itself, in the process of institutionalizing itself, as the primary form of the secularization of the gospel. It is the bodying forth of Christ's Spirit in the world. This is bound to have two sides. On the one hand, it represents the victory of faith which overcomes the world. It is an attempt to refashion life in this present world which, left to itself, becomes increasingly self-contradictory and destructive, after the form of that which is to come. On the other hand, to the extent to which it succeeds in doing this, the body which it has in the world grows in size and becomes exposed to all the corrupting influences which are abroad in the world. All those forces which are not controlled by the Spirit of Christ are able to get to work on it and the more successful the secularization has been—and successful, let it again be emphasized, according to its own criteria of success—the larger and more tempting the target it provides.

Christian maturity demands of us the recognition that this process is inevitable, so that we refuse to be surprised or indignant when it takes place and that we call upon the resources which we have for not succumbing to the dangers of success. A restated doctrine of development of church institutional life, as well as doctrine, is badly needed, one which is based on close observation and which is emancipated from Newman's aesthetic intoxication with the idea, rather than the reality, of Catholicism, and one which also does full justice to the inescapably ambivalent nature of the process of secularization, even in the most favorable circumstances within the context of a civilization calling itself Christendom. This has quite astringently practical consequences. If, for example, in all the time it was discussing "secularization" in general terms, the World Council of Churches had seen this and had looked at itself as one earthly organization among others, in many respects similar to other international agencies which surrounded it in Geneva, it might have prevented itself from moving quite so rapidly in the same direction as many of them, in becoming increasingly elaborate, expensive, bureaucratic, and vulnerable to exploitation by organized pressure groups.[21]

There are two rules, which are already sufficiently clear to have application today, about the way in which the Christian community should develop as one institution among others in the life of the world if it is to avoid going the way of the world. The first is very simple, but failure to see it still gives rise to misplaced concern. Christian growth toward maturity is best judged in qualitative rather than in quantitative terms. It is not the size of the plant but its health, appearance, taste, and power of propagation that matter. This is not to say that, therefore, statistics of membership and of giving are unimportant. Over the long term, if not in the short run, the probability is that a church expanding in these ways is likely to be healthier on more fundamental levels also than one which is steadily shrinking. Yet if the plant is to continue to flourish in the difficult climate of the world, it needs deep roots. The striking of these roots takes time and is not readily visible, and for healthy growth it is more important to nourish the roots than to be efficient in gathering all the fruits. A church which does not strike deeper as her institutional body grows is likely to produce inferior fruit in the next generation and ultimately to wither and die. There is little consolation in seeing the truth of this confirmed in the experience of so many of the churches of popular Protestantism in our own time.

The chief question a church growing toward maturity must be asking itself is not whether it is growing rapidly enough—it could be bolting like a lettuce—but whether its growth is healthy. And this will mean feeding the soil, watering, the ceaseless removal of weeds, and occasional pruning and grafting. It also needs a quality of whose importance no good gardener needs to be reminded: patience. Roman Catholicism has shown this quality in its mission to Western lands in recent generations, but it is one which most forms of Protestantism conspicuously lack. Anyone who compares the position of the Roman church in modern England with what it was a hundred years ago—and the same is partly true in the different circumstances of the USA— will see that such patience is sometimes rewarded even in this life. It is true that occasional *kairoi* do come in the life of institutions as well as of individuals, decisive moments when situations have gathered to a head and when it is essential to move in fast with all that one has to make the most of the opportunity. But Christian growth has usually to start from small beginnings. This is particularly difficult to remember when replanting has to be done on heavily worked soil which has borne good crops in the past. When a plant has grown old, healthy flowers and fruit cannot be maintained without the sowing of fresh seed and going through the long process of maturation. The ground has to be prepared again, and some may have to lie fallow for a time before vigorous growth can be expected.

Without driving the horticultural metaphor too hard, if there is any truth in this kind of analysis it obviously has severely practical impli- cations for church strategy in a country like Britain today, implica- tions which may have relevance for those metropolitan and run-down rural areas of the USA where the churches also languish. One of the troubles with British church life today is that, in the earlier part of this century when previously prosperous churches were beginning to decline, great efforts were made to revive them by church extension and "Forward Movement" schemes. Not enough attention was paid to the replenishment of the ground and to replanting in places where crops had already been gathered. The result is that large areas of British society are left in church life either entirely barren or inhabited only by scrub and stunted second growths.

The second rule is related to the first and is equally simple, although it seems to be equally hard to accept. Because churches must expect to share on the institutional level in the same cycle of growth and decay which other institutions experience and organize themselves to meet without thinking that they are failing when they do so, they must strive always to make realistic appraisals of the points in the cycle at which the various parts of their life are likely to be, and conduct themselves accordingly. Again generalizing broadly, churches in most parts of Britain have to face the problems of institutional late middle age—unlike some other European churches, they do not yet have to face those of senescence. In most parts of the USA—although there are plenty of exceptions, as old-line churches in New England and parts of the South can testify—their problems are those of institutional adolescence. It needs hardly to be said that for institutions to be at an adolescent stage does not carry with it the corollary that the faith of those who belong to them is at the same stage. On the contrary, it is a proof of maturity when members of churches can recognize this about their institutional form, so that they know what problems and opportunities are likely to arise and draw on the experience of the Christian past in meeting them. What matters is that we do our part to help the church "act its age" in God's sight, whether it means moving to the fulfillment or to the restoration of maturity. Only thus can churches overcome the natural tendency of all institutions to reach a peak and then decline, and only thus can they find renewal, even when they are old.

Churches need to remember these things about themselves as they look at themselves as institutions in the setting of the general life of society, but they need also to remember that, as they move out into a wider world, they should become progressively less interested in their own institutional well-being and more and more in that of the world which they claim to serve. This gives a measure of justification to the relative indifference of someone like Reinhold Niebuhr to the relevance of his ideas to the institutional life of churches. From the point of view of his own calling, he could plead that he had more urgent matters to think about. A church is at its most mature when it is forgetting itself in helping the other parts of the life of the community reach their own maturity, as that in its turn is to be understood in a Christian context. This it cannot do unless it gladly recognizes their own autonomy. The other institutions of society are not answerable in the first instance to the church but to God. From this point of view, the American notion of a free church in a free state can be seen as a mature acknowledgment of the need of each for independence from the other if the maturity of each is to be fulfilled. But, to British eyes, the height of the wall of separation built by the Constitution may also prevent sufficient interplay between them.

It is true, however, that experience shows that this relation between churches and the other institutions of society is likely to be most effective when the influence of the one upon the other is indirect. Why this should be so I have tried to work out, with particular reference to the example of educational institutions, in my book, *Beyond Religion.*[22] It is a sign of vitality when a church gives birth to another institution, as it has to many in the course of history. It can do a great deal to nourish and protect that institution in its infancy, but it represents success, not failure, when that institution wants to be independent and to stand on its own feet. A mature church will be thankful that this child is now off its hands and will look around for other useful work to do in the world.[23]

A church that understands what coming of age means will know that it will be weakened and vulnerable itself as long as the other significant institutions of the society in which it is set, and in which many of its own members have to carry responsibility, are immature or in decline. The difficulties confronting churches in modern Britain are not unconnected with a more general weakening of community life and the difficulties in which educational establishments, political parties, industrial firms, families, and even sporting organizations find themselves. They will not be solved by the one in isolation from the others. In a time when they have their own full share of such difficulties, churches will testify most clearly to the fact that they are on the way to maturity by the way in which they cease to be anxious for their own life and aid and support their members as they help other institutions of society to act their own age as those who are responsible in their own place to their Creator.

Notes

CHAPTER 1

1. SCM Press, 2nd ed, 1971, pp. 56–9. All following references are to this edition.
2. "Since the issue of events then, success, is in the hands not of men but of God, the pilot of history, it is not a cowardly opportunism, but the truly fruitful relation to history, when we, whether as victors or vanquished, turn our attention to historical success and attribute ethical relevance to it" (*Reality and Faith*, vol. 1, Lutterworth Press, Guilford, Surrey, 1971, p. 301). What that ethical relevance might be we are not told.
3. G. C. Berkouwer, *The Triumph of Grace in the Theology of Karl Barth*, Paternoster Press, Exeter, Devon, 1956.
4. There are a few pages about success near the end of *Church Dogmatics* IV.3.ii, pp. 747–51 (T. & T. Clark, Edinburgh, 1962), but they are chiefly concerned with the church's lack of worldly success and with the attitude it should show in the face of this apparent failure.
5. This is not to deny, of course, that the gospel is good news, first of all, to the poor and that it cannot be properly received until we are aware of how impoverished we are without it. But once we receive Christ, we are rich.
6. Eph. 4:13 (RSV).
7. Notably in *Church Dogmatics* III.1, pp. 288–89.
8. Eph. 4:14 (NEB). It is ironical that Nietzsche should have come to regard Christian spokesmen as, in effect, such rogues and schemers, producing a morality for slaves which justifies failure.
9. See the discussion of "The Concrete Place" in Bonhoeffer, *Ethics*, pp. 66ff.
10. Mark 7:27–9.
11. I have tried to work out some of its implications for the Christian community in my own country in my book *The British: Their Identity and Their Religion* (SCM Press, London, 1975). If I resist the temptation to

discuss this theme with reference to the "liberation theology" propounded by South American and other so-called "Third World" theologians, it is not because I do not recognize its importance, or the fact that it has implications for Christian responsibility in my own situation, but because my own identification with the situations out of which it has arisen is, as yet, so inadequate that any comments I might have to make about it are unlikely to have much pertinence.

12. This is a point brought out well in Robert M. Brown's *New Frontiers for the Church Today,* Oxford University Press, 1974.

13. It is moving to see how this sometimes works even with such natural egotists as professional politicians. Presidents Truman and Johnson are two such who appear to have been awed into humility by the burdens of their great office, with self-justification reasserting its familiar sway only after they had served their terms and begun to write their memoirs.

14. Phil. 2:6.

15. "It is arguably not the Attilas who ride through blood to a throne and maintain their rule by merciless oppression, who achieve the deepest and most perilous domination over their fellows. 'What shall it profit a man if he gain the whole world and lose his own soul?' The man who should strain his ears to catch that most searching question is not the man who has enlarged his resources by enterprises as savagely concluded as they were ruthlessly conceived and executed. Rather it is the man whom his fellows with good reason acclaim as their benefactor, who indeed has, almost unknown to himself, enlarged his private image both of himself and his role by singularly generous service to others," D. M. Mackinnon, *The Problem of Metaphysics,* Cambridge University Press, 1974, p. 140.

CHAPTER 2

1. He criticizes Bach's St. Matthew Passion for failing to bring this out sufficiently (*Church Dogmatics* IV.2, pp. 252f.). In this he may not be entirely fair, because the note of victory is more pronounced in St. Luke than in St. Matthew, but it is a reasonable comment on the sentimentally pietist libretto Bach used for his choruses, chorales and arias.

2. Jacques Ellul, *Violence,* SCM Press, London, 1969.

3. Matt. 5:10–12.

4. Phil. 4:4–7.

5. In his book *Enough Is Enough* (SCM Press, 1975, pp. 45–6), John Taylor claims that *epieikeia* derives from the same root as ikon, a likeness, and that it also has the sense of a matching, a tuning in with the whole, relating to the way in which all things fit together, cohere, in Christ.

6. See, in particular, *The Children of Light and the Children of Darkness,* Scribners, New York, 1944.

7. This is not the place to inquire into all that the apostle meant by his expectation that the Lord was near. What can be said is that it did not mean

indifference to what happens here and now, but a sharpened awareness of moral realities.

8. *Church Dogmatics* III.2, p. 47.

9. Luke 1:52.

10. 2 Cor. 14:16–18.

11. Rom. 5:3–5.

12. This is something which was always clearly recognized in the classical English educational tradition. See also Bonhoeffer on "The Natural Rights of the Life of the Mind," and in particular the sketch of the unfinished section on page 159 of *Ethics*.

CHAPTER 3

1. Dean Kelly, in his interesting book, *Why Conservative Churches Are Growing* (Harper & Row, New York, 1972, p. 55), quotes what he calls Wesley's Law: "Wherever riches have increased, the essence of religion has increased in the same proportion. Therefore, I do not see how it is possible, in the nature of things, for any revival of religion to continue long. For religion must necessarily produce industry and frugality and these cannot but produce riches. But as riches increase so will pride, anger and love of the world in all its branches."

2. The tercentenary of the death of John Milton was celebrated in London in the autumn of 1974. Nothing is more unbecoming than to pass superficial moral judgments on the great figures of the past. Our first debt to Milton is one of gratitude for his mighty achievements and any query concerning possible failings must be qualified by a recognition of the difficulties he had to face— the frustration caused by his blindness, the intensification by circumstances of the isolation which all creative artists need and his disappointment at the failure of the good old cause of the English Revolution, in which he passionately believed. Yet he does appear to have been partly infected by the spiritual pride he so vividly described in Satan, a pride which, for example, made him lose sympathy even before the Restoration with the struggles of Cromwell as he was faced with the practical necessities of government. It has been said that Milton was an independent churchman in a church of one member, but that is no church at all because one is not an ecclesiastical quorum.

3. Oxford University Press, 1939.

4. To say this is not to imply any disparagement of the nonslothful elements in the religion and culture of the South and East, from whose traditions the Protestant North may have a great deal to learn.

CHAPTER 4

1. This provides whatever measure of justification exists for the strictures of Dr. E. R. Norman on the attitudes of many Christian spokespersons in his

Reith Lectures on *Christianity and the World Order* (Oxford University Press, 1979), although it cannot excuse the unbalanced and ill-informed way in which the criticism is made.

2. Rom. 8:19. See the striking article, "A Civilisation of Technics" by Philip Mairet in *A Prospect for Christendom,* ed. Maurice B. Reckitt (Faber & Faber, 1944).

CHAPTER 5

1. Knopf, New York, 1964.

2. See Karl Barth, *Church Dogmatics* III. 4, pp. 390ff. (T. & T. Clark, Edinburgh, 1961).

3. All published in translation by the SCM Press, London, in 1967, 1974 and 1977 respectively, and by Harper & Row in America.

4. *Letters and Papers from Prison,* enlarged edition (SCM Press, London, 1971), pp. 360–61.

5. *Dietrich Bonhoeffer* by Eberhard Bethge (Collins Publishers, London, 1970), p. 780.

CHAPTER 6

1. "Jesus comes before man with complete assurance and resolute authority. He teaches directly, without seeking to cover himself; he acts as the moment demands, not by precedent. Like a king, he summons men to follow him; and he challenges the scribes to combat as if he himself had absolutely no need of rabbinic instruction . . . . He acts with complete freedom as the person he is, and thus, in this comprehensive sense, with authority."—Hans Von Campenhausen, *Ecclesiastical Authority and Spiritual Power in the Church of the First Three Centuries,* A. & C. Black London, 1969, p. 4.

2. See the illuminating discussion in G. B. Caird, *Principalities and Powers* (Oxford University Press, 1956) of the changing role of Satan in Scripture, where he is transformed from being an agent to being an enemy of God's purpose. Caird suggests that the reason for this is that Satan, originally the guardian of God's consequent will that sinners should suffer punishment, absolutized this and thus became a barrier to the vocation of Jesus, which was one of restoring us to grace. Caird draws a parallel in the changing role of the law in Paul's teaching (Chapter 2, "The Great Accuser," pp. 31–53).

3. John 6:66–68. Peter's reply ("Lord, to whom shall we go? Thou hast the words of eternal life") could be interpreted as saying in effect, "There is nothing we should like more, but where can we go? You have stirred up in us a need for true and enduring life, which only you are able to satisfy."

4. It may be of more significance than Christians of most traditions would care to contemplate that in the fourth Gospel, possibly written two generations after the event, even the words of institution are omitted from the account of the Supper. We are given instead the acted parable of the washing of the disciples' feet, together with a very heavy underlining of its meaning for

the way in which they are to exercise authority. This suggests—and the suggestion is given added force when the context in which Paul repeats the words of institution in 1 Cor. 11:23–25 is recalled—that even at that early date the Lord's Supper was in danger of being transformed into an occasion for expressing worldly privilege and power, so that the evangelist needed to recall his readers very sharply to its real meaning.

5. See Barth's great excursus on Judas in *Church Dogmatics* II.2. He sees Judas's "handing over" of Jesus as the negative parallel to the Pauline *paradosis,* the "handing over" of the knowledge of the saving acts of faith. Barth says that even Judas's betrayal is used as a true *paradosis* because, by the placing of Jesus in the hands of the powers of this world, Jesus is able, by showing their powerlessness to hold him even though he surrenders all earthly power, to assert his redeeming power over us.

6. Karl Barth, *Credo* (Hodder & Stoughton Sevenoaks, Kent, 1937), p. 87.

7. *Ibid.* There may be no incompatibility between the cry of dereliction in Matthew and Mark and the quieter and apparently more positive cry in Luke, "Father, into thy hands I commend my spirit" (Luke 23:46). This could be interpreted as saying that his work, including his rejection, being accomplished, there is now nothing left for him but to hand his spirit back to God, since humankind had no more use for him. Like the cry of dereliction, it throws into all the sharper relief the transformation of the resurrection and the first coming of the Spirit.

CHAPTER 7

1. Eberhard Jüngel, *Death: The Riddle and the Mystery* (St. Andrew Press, Edinburgh, 1975).

2. The richness of these relationships and the profundity of common experience to which they led was well brought out in Lionel Thornton's impressive book, *The Common Life in the Body of Christ* (Dacre Press, London, 1944).

CHAPTER 8

1. Faber & Faber, London, 1965.

CHAPTER 9

1. See especially his *The Point of View of my Work as an Author,* Oxford University Press, 1939.

2. In *Church Dogmatics,* in various parts of the vast Vol. III, especially III.1, ch. 45 of III.2, and III.4.

3. Barth reminds us, as many others have before him, that Don Juan is not the hero but the weakling, the hopelessly immature person, in the matter of love.

4. Bonhoeffer, following the Lutheran tradition, does the same when he speaks of marriage as one of what he calls the four mandates (*Ethics,* pp. 179–84). He was denied the opportunity of saying much about it, but what hints he gives suggest a surprisingly conservative attitude.

5. After all, there are many aspects of that same past, such as the way in which patriarchs and kings in Israel took polygamy for granted, which few Christians today would think it right to emulate.

6. 1 John 3:2 (RSV).

7. Eph. 4:4–6.

8. *Church Dogmatics* III.4, p. 167.

9. III.2, p. 287.

10. It is appropriate to refer again at this point to the remarkable section in the *Dogmatics* III.1, pp. 288–329, and also to his highly contentious claim, based on his exegesis of Pauline teaching, that this order of precedence still has its place in the Christian dispensation (*Dogmatics* III.2, pp. 301–16 and III.4, pp. 172–76).

11. See Barth, III.4, pp. 176–81, on masculine "strength" and feminine "maturity." What he says may describe a continuing factor in relations between men and women but, on his own showing, should there not be a kind of mutual influence of their characteristic attributes at their best, as men and women grow in grace?

CHAPTER 10

1. "The adolescent as a distinct species is the creation of modern social attitudes and institutions. A creature neither child nor adult, he is a comparatively recent socio-psychological invention, scarcely two centuries old. Distinctive social institutions have been fashioned to accommodate him; in psychology he has been made more or less to fit them, moulded by appropriate rewards and penalties" (Frank Musgrove, *Youth and the Social Order,* Routledge & Kegan Paul, London, 1964, p. 13).

2. Expressed even more tendentiously in Professor Musgrove's more recent book on a similar theme, *Patterns of Power and Authority in English Education,* Routledge & Kegan Paul, London, 1971.

3. Cambridge University Press, 1972.

4. See Matt. 11:30.

5. Perhaps professors should cease to head their departments not later than the age of sixty, taking instead a more functional and less merely honorific emeritus status. And if the Reformed churches are ever to surrender to the Episcopalian demand that they "take episcopacy into their system," it would only be tolerable from their point of view if bishops ceased to be the font and focus of church order but became instead dignified semiretired ministers, available for counsel and for taking part in representative occasions but with little executive power and a firm understanding that, in the ordinary way, no new leadership is to be expected from them.

CHAPTER 11

1. See in particular Horst Symanowski, *The Christian Witness in an Industrial Society,* Collins Publishers, London, 1966.

2. Doubleday, New York, 1961.

3. See Alexander Miller, *Christian Vocation in the Contemporary World,* SCM Press, London, 1947. The same is broadly true of Catholic theology influenced by Marxism. A different approach was made by the Anglo-Catholic Christendom group, who were influential in England a generation ago, of which T. S. Eliot was a prominent member. See V. A. Demant, "Vocation in Work" in *Theology of Society,* Faber, 1946, pp. 175–84 and M. B. Reckitt, "Work in the Crisis of our Culture" in *Our Culture* ed. V. A. Demant, SPCK, London, 1947, pp. 70–96.

4. In *Church Dogmatics* III.4.iii, "The Active Life," pp. 470–564.

5. This reminds me of an observation in one of Van Gogh's letters, when he explains that his drawing of a loom is different from a straightforward design print because he has to convey the sense of the struggle of the hand involved in using the loom.

6. This is discussed at greater length in the chapter on "Incomes and Standards of Living" in my *Equality and Excellence,* SCM Press, London, 1961.

7. We have to remember that the rich young ruler was the representative of Israel, which had allowed the possessions she enjoyed as the fruit of faith, her law and the common life she enjoyed in obedience to the law, to become a barrier in the way of the fulfillment of her vocation.

8. It was the economist Pigou who pointed out many years ago the self-defeating character of the pursuit of luxury. The satisfaction derived from lesser luxuries diminishes as greater ones become possible. At one stage, to have any car seems to be the height of luxury, but who is content with a Volkswagen when he might possibly own a Rolls Royce?

9. See E. F. Schumacher, *Small Is Beautiful,* Abacus Books, Tunbridge Wells, Kent, 1974.

10. It was a Protestant romantic who conspicuously failed to understand the Reformation, Thomas Carlyle, who preached the doctrine, *laborare est orare.*

11. It is hard to accept comparisons between the allegedly joyless character of play in modern Protestant lands devoted to football, baseball, and cricket, in contrast to that in Latin countries whose chief contribution to sport is the bullfight.

12. This partly explains why so many great creators, especially artists, have rarely achieved widespread recognition in their own lifetimes. It is only nowadays, with improved medicine, that some of them are able to live on long enough after their main creative periods are over to begin to collect some of the rewards.

In reading Welsh history recently I was struck by the way in which, at the time when, in the first half of the nineteenth century, the modern Welsh nation was being formed and the materially poor Welsh countryside was bursting with fresh cultural and political vitality, which matured in later generations and sometimes on distant soil, their great hymns were full of longing for the world to come and their Sundays were savored as prefigurements of eternity. See *Welsh Rural Communities* ed. Elwyn Davies and Alwyn D. Rees, University of Wales Press, Cathays, Cardiff, 1960, pp. 198–99.

13. Some highly successful, and no less highly rewarded, sports professionals make an open confession of their piety and say that it helps their performance. Their witness would be more impressive if it led them sometimes to take light-hearted, and expensive, risks, just for fun, to underline the fact that all this is only a form of play. Professionalism is the clericalism of sport and needs to safeguard itself against the moral ambiguities of all clericalism.

CHAPTER 12

1. Dietrich Bonhoeffer, *Letters and Papers from Prison,* enlarged edition, (SCM Press, London, 1971), pp. 326ff.

2. See in particular the chapter on "Christ, Reality and Good" (subtitled "Christ, the Church and the World") in *Ethics,* pp. 161–84. What one wonders, in the light of his later observations in *Letters and Papers,* is whether he would still have been content with the highly conservative Lutheran interpretation he gives of the "mandates" in the last part of that section as he considered further the implications of his unitive concept of reality.

3. This, of course, will be hotly contested by modern pluralism, some of whose more radical exponents would doubt whether it even makes much sense to speak at all of anything as definite as human nature, while others, with a more positive point of view, argue that it rules out the possibility of learning valuable things about human nature from other religions and philosophies than the Christian one. If this possibility were ruled out, then clearly the Christian claim would need to be restated in such a way as to bring it back in again, because all human experience must be relevant in some way to the understanding of maturity, and the claim it makes for itself must be treated with full seriousness. And it is more essential than ever in these days that Christians should realize that our true nature is only in the process of being revealed as we move to meet the coming Christ, bearing all in human experience that can endure his scrutiny with us. It is not something simply given to the church, and given to the church as one historical community among others. Once again, it "doth not yet appear what we shall be." What we do know is that "when he shall appear, we shall be like him; for we shall see him as he is" (1 John 3:2).

4. See the distinction made by Bonhoeffer between "hopeless godless-

ness" within the church and "promising godlessness" outside it (*Ethics*, p. 83).

5. *Man's Disorder and God's Design* ed., John C. Bennett, SCM Press, London, 1947.

6. One of the troubles with the Western world today is that a great deal of this adolescent vitality has been channeled into vastly expanded academic institutions. This has now excessively prolonged the period of adolescence, denying real responsibility to people who are more than ready for it and need its discipline, while churches and other institutions which could do with this vitality are prevented from receiving it.

7. Eph. 4.15.

8. This is vividly conveyed by Masaccio's "Baptism of the Neophytes" in the Carmine church in Florence.

9. The Lutheran tradition has, perhaps, suffered even more. It is disconcerting to find Bonhoeffer, even as late as the *Ethics*, stating a sharply clericalist position on this matter, with only a faint gesture in the direction of the necessary distinction and qualifications. "The book of homilies and the prayer-book are the principal books for the congregation; the Holy Scripture is the book for the preacher; there can be little doubt that this formulation correctly represents the divinely ordained relationship between the congregation and the office" (p. 261). Can there not indeed? Even so relatively conservative a Roman Catholic theologian as Karl Rahner would cast doubt on it in these days. See his *Theology of Pastoral Action*, Burns & Oates, London, 1968, pp. 60–63.

10. Paul makes this point precisely in his discussion of gifts and offices in 1 Cor. 12.

11. Eph. 4:11–12.

12. And the sensible minister will take due note of the fact that Aaron, with his "gift of the gab," was a sufficiently insecure and dubious character. No doubt because he was uncertain of his "role" and sought reassurance of his own "relevance," it was he who decided, while Moses was tiresomely absent communing with God on Sinai, that there was no alternative but to meet "the expressed needs of his people" and to supervise the organization of the worship of the Golden Calf.

13. 1 Cor. 2:6.

14. It is a defect in Hans Küng's otherwise admirable book *Why Priests?* (Collins Fontana, London, 1972) that he still seems to see the ministry primarily in terms of "leadership."

15. In view of this, one wonders whether Bonhoeffer would have wanted to continue to defend the conception of the relation between minister and people already quoted from the *Ethics*, especially in the light of his further reflections on the world come of age and speaking to man in his strength.

16. Lay theologians, says one of them, must

    1. Be able to read the Bible intelligently.

2. Have a general understanding of what Christian doctrine is and why they believe it on the level of an educated and scholarly adult.

3. Have a knowledge of what is really going on in the world and of what Christian responsibility in public affairs involves.

4. Have devoted thought to the Christian implications and demands of their own profession, including facing honestly whether it has a right to exist at all.

(W. H. Moberly, *The Crisis in the University,* SCM Press, London, 1948, pp. 269–70)

This sees things too much in terms of the professional person or public servant—there could be other lay theologians whose vocation lay in very different directions—but it is on the right lines.

17. Most of the creative work of the world has been in the form of unpaid service. This is no argument for not paying ministers, as Paul, himself an unpaid minister, acknowledged, but it is a reason for showing a certain detachment over the whole matter of payment, together with great sensitivity concerning the terms of the relationship where payment is involved.

18. The essays by Wolf-Dieter Marsch, Frederick A. Shippey, and Walter G. Muelder in *Institutionalism and Church Unity,* ed. Nils Ehrenstrom and Walter G. Muelder, SCM Press, London, 1963, are refreshing exceptions.

19. SCM Press, London, 1963.

20. Ernst Käsemann, *Perspectives on Paul,* SCM Press, London, 1971.

21. Such a doctrine of development might also be of help to the theology of "development" in another sense, which is being rightly much discussed in World Council circles today, that of the assumptions on which, and the way in which, so-called programs of "development" in relation to those countries which are supposed to need it, are proceeding.

22. SCM Press, London, 1962.

23. This does not mean, however, that the church should wash its hands of such children. A continuing relationship that is careful to respect the independence which is a corollary of the maturity of each, may be necessary to the health of both. Once again, however, their very success can create barriers. American theological education provides an example of this. In the past relations between churches, colleges, and universities were often creative, even if sometimes in tension, because they had a close relation to each other. The values of the church community had influence upon those of the university and the pulpit was often so imbued with university ideals that it became a significant center for university extension. Its role in awakening an ambition to give higher education to their children among nonacademic people, without which America's phenomenal academic expansion would never have got off the ground, is still inadequately appreciated. But the successful growth of both churches and universities has meant a great increase in the size of both. The result is that it becomes more and more difficult for people, even in theological schools, to have feet in both camps. Each is so big and all-absorbing as to demand full-time and generally lifelong service, and lack of

contact increases mutual suspicion and fear, while both suffer from the lack of candid friends who are detached from their day-to-day affairs but on whose judgment, and loyalty, they can rely. It is not surprising, therefore, that their recent success is already beginning to produce evidence of new pride, complacency, and sloth in some parts of each set of institutions.